Mart.
Tel:

Managing
ICT

Terry Freedman
Series Editor: Professor Trevor Kerry

Note on Series Editor

Professor Trevor Kerry is well known for his books on the practice of teaching. He was formerly a senior LEA Adviser in charge of in-service training, and more recently has been a consultant and lecturer on aspects of education management. He holds a Visiting Fellowship in the University of East Anglia, and is a Vice-President of the College of Teachers. He sustains his contact with the classroom by teaching on a regular basis and is an Ofsted trained inspector.

Orders: please contact Bookpoint Ltd, 39 Milton Park, Abingdon, Oxon OX14 4TD. Telephone: (44) 01235 400414, Fax: (44) 01235 400454. Lines are open from 9.00 – 6.00, Monday to Saturday, with a 24 hour message answering service. Email address: orders@bookpoint.co.uk

British Library Cataloguing in Publication Data
A catalogue record for this title is available from The British Library.

ISBN 0 340 75334 X

First published 1999
Impression number   10 9 8 7 6 5 4 3 2 1
Year   2005 2004 2003 2002 2001 2000 1999

Typeset by Transet Limited, Coventry, England.
Printed in Great Britain for Hodder & Stoughton Educational, a division of Hodder Headline Plc, 338 Euston Road, London NW1 3BH by Cox & Wyman, Reading, Berkshire

Contents

Statement of principles

The books in this series are based on a particular philosophy of teaching, which was largely developed (but not fossilised) in the 1980s as a result of the Teacher Education Project in the Universities of Nottingham, Leicester and Exeter – of which the series editor was Co-ordinator. This philosophy has stood the test of time and, it is argued, better meets the needs of teachers as professionals than some more recent developments, such as some competence models, which tend to trivialise the art and science of teaching. The principles of this philosophy are as stated:

Practical teaching consists of skills

- Skills can be isolated and identified
- Skills can be broken down into component parts
- Skills can be studied and taught
- Skills can be learned
- Skills can be reflected upon and refined
- Skills can be evaluated and assessed.

Each book takes a particular teaching skill and uses the latest research and practice to illuminate it in ways of immediate interest to all teachers.

Editorial: Skills for the future

The pace of change in society is constantly accelerating. This change is reflected in the world of education. Indeed, Drucker sums it up like this:

> *Every few hundred years in Western history there occurs a sharp transformation ... Within a few short decades, society re-arranges itself – its worldview; its basic values; its social and political structures; its arts, its key institutions. Fifty years later, there is a new world ... We are currently living through such a transformation.*
>
> **(Drucker, P (1993) Post-Capitalist Society. New York: Harper Business, p1)**

> *What will be taught and learned; how it will be taught and learned; who will make use of schooling; and the position of the school in society – all of this will change greatly during ensuing decades. Indeed, no other institution faces changes as radical as those that will transform the school.*
>
> **(Drucker, op. cit. p209)**

Yet it could be argued that even these changes have been modest in scope and pace compared with the changes that are likely to occur in the early years of the twenty-first century. Already the portents are visible of events which may affect radically *Schools for the Future*. These are just some of the changes of the recent past:

- the advent of the new learning technologies
- consumer choice and its implications for schools
- a re-definition of the nature of schools in the education process
- the changing place of Britain in the global economy and in the development of global markets
- concerns about environmental issues and the use of resources
- re-valuation of the place of non-teaching staff in the education process
- the pressure to achieve 'more for the same' brought about by budgetary constraints and increased emphasis on targets and performance measures.

So how should schools be responding to these challenges, and what can be done to support them?

School responses

Schools are already exploring solutions for a changing world. Some of these approaches can be broadly categorised as follows:

Increasing the emphasis on learning

Traditionally, the world of education has concentrated on teaching, making the assumption that learning will follow inevitably. However, the emphasis of the late 1980s and the 1990s on assessing and recording standards of achievement has forced a re-thinking of this simplistic view. Students' learning rather than teachers' teaching is increasingly seen to be at the crux of the education process: the emphasis has moved from inputs to outcomes.

Re-aligning teachers to be 'directors of learning'

The increasing emphasis on the process of learning has caused many schools, and teachers themselves, to review the teaching function. Teachers often now conceptualise their roles more in terms of 'directors of learning' than as purveyors of teaching. The change is a subtle one which does not deny the traditional 'art and science' of teaching; but it concentrates more on the use of those skills to bring about learning in the student.

Assessing the implications of the new technologies

Among the most powerful resources which teachers, as directors of learning, have at their disposal is the developing technology bound up in Information Technology. This opens up entirely new avenues of communication, making access to data simple, self-study a powerful tool, and availability of information international.

Extending teachers' roles to be managers of the learning environment in its widest sense

Old-fashioned concepts of 'one teacher, one class' for primary schools, or of 'one subject specialist, one class' in the secondary sector are, in the scenario we have painted, as redundant in the twenty-first century as Victorian pupil-monitors are today. The teachers of the future may exercise less of a role in class control or in the traditional skills of exposition: they may well be the programme-makers and resource creators of the future. They will not 'do the teaching', they will manage (in every sense) the intellectual environment that students will inhabit.

Reappraising patterns of learning

One of the implications of the picture painted here is that not only will teachers' roles and patterns of working change, but so will those of the learners. With more and more computers home-based, even portable, not all learning will need to take place in schools as they are currently modelled. The purposes of school buildings and their patterns of use will become subject to reappraisal.

What must we do?

Education stands at a cross-roads. One of the ways in which some educationists are dealing with this is to establish projects, such as the *Schools for the Future* project with which I have been involved at the University of Lincolnshire and Humberside. The project is primarily intended to support developments and changes for this twenty-first century world. It is attempting to do this in a number of ways, as shown below.

Through an analysis of change as it affects education

The project will be alert for, and seek out, the global and national trends in education which are likely to affect schools and learning in the immediate future.

Through research into innovative practice

In particular, the project will seek out innovative practice, large- or small-scale, in Britain and overseas. Whenever possible, we will try to explore at first hand not just the problems and their solutions, but the decision-making processes and creative approaches which have been used.

Through a specific research project on the use of school time and plant

The project team is already involved with a Funding Agency project in a group of schools in London. Here we are experimenting with one of the fundamental issues to face *Schools for the Future*: the structure of the school day and the school year. This is a collaborative venture located in three schools in which we shall be monitoring and evaluating not only the outcomes (in terms of new patterns of attendance and their effects), but also the kinds of radical thinking which are used to arrive at solutions.

Through an examination of the developing uses of new technologies in schools

One of the keys to future developments in education will, inevitably, be the uses to which new technologies are put. These are already developing as a powerful tool for communication, and to a lesser extent for learning. These parallel developments are set to continue; and the ways in which they are adopted into, and woven into the fabric of, educational provision in the future are potentially very challenging to traditional thinking about schools and their functions. The project will seek to explore both innovation in this field, and to speculate about alternative models of learning.

Through an examination of the decision-making processes and mind-sets needed to bring about dramatic change

This project is about dramatic, rather than marginal, change. In the project's studies of innovative practice we shall be as concerned with the thinking process leading to change as with the change itself. These are largely uncharted waters, and we shall be breaking new ground in exploring this issue – which may have implications for the selection and education of leaders for the future.

Through dissemination of best practice

A fundamental purpose of this project will be to pass on to the education world the lessons which we are able to learn. We shall do this through whatever channels are most appropriate: visits, courses, conferences, books, journal articles, in-service training events, the Internet and the media. Our main concern will not be to provide examples of practice which others may copy directly in their own situations, but to tease out the principles which others may apply to reach their own conclusions in their unique situations.

What are the broad philosophies behind the project?

Schools for the Future is based on the principles of reengineering. Michael Hammer defines reengineering as:

> *The fundamental rethinking and radical redesign of business processes to bring about dramatic improvements in performance.*
> **(Hammer, M and Champy, P (1997) The Reengineering Revolution Handbook. *New York: Harper Business, p3*)**

At the heart of the reengineering philosophy is the client/customer. Reengineering is about providing a better service in a changing environment; but it is more than tinkering with structures to achieve marginally more acceptable results. Reengineering uses the best insights from other management theories (team-work, total quality management, etc.), but is much more than the sum of these parts. It is a mind-set that uses creative thinking in a focused way to achieve quite different ways of working. It is anticipatory rather than reactive.

Reengineering and teaching skills

This series of books of teaching skills has developed out of my interest in reengineering as well as from my long-term involvement with the initial and in-service training of teachers. Part of the intention of the series is to identify those traditional teaching skills which will continue to be fundamental to the teacher in the twenty-first century, and to provide a means of support for those who wish to acquire or improve them. Thus class management is likely to remain a fundamental skill for teachers: but its nature will change to accommodate the new roles for teachers as directors of learning and as managers of para-professionals in the classroom. However, other skills, such as the exploitation of the new technologies, are of recent origin and will have to be assimilated by all teachers, including those who perhaps trained for a school system which operated rather differently in the recent past.

Education is changing rapidly; and the nature of the teacher's job is changing, too. Some people find change only negative and disturbing. This series treats change as a positive phenomenon: one which challenges and excites. Hopefully, these books do not lose sight of traditional wisdom nor of the continuing values of which the profession is rightly proud. But they do look forward in a spirit of progression and development to where schools are going rather than to where they have been.

Professor Trevor Kerry
Series Editor

About this book

It is now widely recognised that information and communications technology (ICT) has a key role to play in schools and colleges. As well as preparing pupils for the world of work, ICT can be used to enhance all areas of the curriculum, while the study of information technology (IT) in its own right can raise pupils' problem-solving abilities.

However, changing the curriculum to incorporate IT and ICT, and even pouring lots of money into resources, are not in themselves sufficient for achieving the benefits of using computers in the curriculum. The key element in making it all work is good management, and that is the focus of this book.

This book provides an extensive resource for the manager of ICT, whether that person is an ICT Co-ordinator, head of department or a senior manager, and whether or not they are new in the post. It has been designed to be useful at primary, secondary and college levels. It will also prove useful for trainee teachers considering a career in teaching IT and/or managing ICT.

The book does not have to be read sequentially (although it may be), but is designed to be dipped into for reference as the need arises.

It would not have been feasible to attempt to produce a book that gave all the answers in the ever-changing world of ICT. Hopefully, this book provides many of the questions. As far as possible, the focus is on management rather that the issues themselves, because although the circumstances or the technology may change quite rapidly, basic management considerations tend to change rather more slowly. A case in point is the discussion about ways of delivering IT. Rather than become involved in the advantages and disadvantages of different approaches in terms of their effect on achievement, the discussion centres on the implications of each approach from the standpoint of ease of management.

A note on terminology

These days, many people are using the term 'ICT' rather than 'IT', where the 'C' stands for Communications. This is clearly an extremely important area, because computer and communications technologies are becoming more and more intertwined with each passing day.

At this point it's worth considering what the term 'ICT' actually means. The National Curriculum Programme of Study specifies the teaching of IT, not ICT. Moreover, there have been at least three different interpretations of what the letters 'ICT' stand for.

A useful distinction between the two terms has been adopted by the Qualifications and Curriculum Authority (QCA) and Department for Education and Employment (DfEE) in their Primary IT scheme of work:

> *Information and communicating technologies (ICT) are the computing and communications facilities and features that variously support teaching, learning and a range of activities in education.*
>
> ...
>
> *The focus is on the subject being taught or studied, or the organisation being administered, rather than developing pupils' skills with, and knowledge of, the technologies themselves.*
>
> *Information technology (IT) comprises the knowledge, skills and understanding needed to employ information and communications technologies appropriately, securely and fruitfully in learning, employment and everyday life. IT is to ICT as literacy is to books, journals or screen displays. The focus on IT is on pupils' capability with ICT ...*
>
> **(Information Technology, A scheme of work for Key Stages 1 and 2, QCA/DfEE, 1998)**

At the time of writing this book, the indications were that this was the terminology to be adopted in the next version of the National Curriculum, due to be implemented in September 2000. However, after the book had been completed the consultation documents for the proposed new National Curriculum were published. One of the issues raised in the proposals are whether the term 'ICT' should be adopted more or less universally, and the term 'IT' dropped apart from its use in some qualifications. Furthermore, the 'C' in 'ICT' in the proposals stands for 'communication' rather than 'communications'. This has led to a renewal of the ICT vs. IT debate within the educational IT community, and it is impossible to predict what the favoured term will be.

Fortunately, any changes in these areas will not affect the advice given here. Even if the subject is renamed ICT, the distinction drawn between IT and ICT in this book (see below) will not detract from the guidance contained in these pages.

Throughout this book, I have used the term 'IT' to refer to the subject or body of knowledge known as Information Technology. For the most part, however, I have adopted the term 'ICT' to refer to both the hardware and software, and its use in the curriculum.

Where the term 'ICT manager' appears, it may be taken to mean Head of IT, or IT or ICT Co-ordinator: the possible meanings should be obvious from the context in which the phrase appears.

Because of the clumsiness of referring to 'pupils and students', and 'teachers and lecturers', I have mostly used the terms 'pupils' and 'staff' or 'teachers' respectively.

Acknowledgements

I should like to thank the following people who have given generously of their time in reading through draft copies of this book, and pointing out errors of fact or omission. Needless to say, sole responsibility for any remaining errors lies with myself.

Mark Adams, for drawing my attention to typographical errors and inconsistencies; Andrew Bush, for providing many insights and examples, particularly in respect of Key Stages 1 and 2; Elaine Freedman, for attention to details such as spelling and grammatical errors and inconsistencies, and for internet research; Graham Marshment for useful suggestions and general encouragement; and Pippa Ray-Adams, for numerous suggestions about the wording and suggestions relating to primary school teaching.

The following people kindly supplied information about resources available on the internet:

Caroline Briggs, Sonia Crisp, Nancy Kunnemann, Karen Lunsford, Mark Magennis, Sanford E. Morris, Craig Nansen, John Potter (who also made some useful suggestions), Kathy Riikonen, Gleason Sackman, Mark Sealey, Rusty Sinclair, Michele Sokoloff, Mathy Vanbuel.

I should also like to thank the following people for permission to reproduce quotations from published material:

Carolyn Ford, of BECTa; Roger Luxton OBE, Principal Inspector, Barking and Dagenham LEA; and Sir Dennis Stevenson.

Chapter 1
Personal skills

Introduction

This chapter looks at the types of skills you need in order to be a successful manager of ICT. There is no magic combination of teaching and computing skills, but some of the content of this chapter may surprise you.

The history of computing is characterised by the movement of computing from the realm of the technician to the domain of the ordinary person. Consequently, technical knowledge is no longer as important as other kinds of knowledge and skills for managing ICT. This is not to say that technical knowledge is unimportant, but that it is the total combination of skills and knowledge that counts.

Types of knowledge

There are four main areas of knowledge to consider:

- hardware knowledge;
- software knowledge;
- curriculum knowledge;
- general knowledge.

Hardware knowledge

You need to:

- have a good understanding of how a computer works;
- be able to refer to parts of the computer by their correct names;
- have a good idea of the strengths and weaknesses of rival hardware platforms and suppliers;
- have a basic understanding of networking terminology, such as 'hub'.

These requirements arise for three main reasons:

- *trouble-shooting* – for example, if you know what happens when you switch a computer on, you will have a better idea of what to look for if nothing happens when you do so;
- *teaching* – it is vitally important to ensure that pupils use the correct terminology from the start, and not use words like 'telly' to refer to the monitor;
- *management* – for example, an understanding of networks gives you a greater chance of obtaining best value when buying one.

There are some aspects of computer hardware that are changing too rapidly for you to really get to know them, unless you have a particular interest in those areas.

For example, communications technology is changing almost by the minute, and is highly technical. It is therefore unrealistic to imagine that the average full-time teacher could keep up to date in this area.

However, you need to be able to discuss options with suppliers, suggest courses of action to the Governing Body or Senior Management Team, and perhaps be able to understand the recommendations of a third party such as a consultant or an LEA advisor.

To be able to do so, you need to keep abreast of developments by reading the specialist magazines, or even simply by keeping a watching brief on the daily newspapers, which often have special features on telecommunications, computer networking and other complex matters. It would also be a good idea to invest in a fairly technical book which covers the principles of computer hardware.

You also need to know how to use all the facets of the internet: the world wide web, newsgroups, mailing lists and, of course, email. Finally, you should know how to set up and maintain a web site. This skill is becoming increasingly essential both for practical reasons, like making documents accessible to all, and what might be called 'marketing' reasons.

Software knowledge

Fortunately, the days when each program worked in a radically different way from every other program are almost over. This means that once you have become familiar with one program you should be able to find your way around another without too much difficulty.

Therefore, as a manager of ICT you do not need to know how every program works, but you should have a good working knowledge of what's available.

For example, you should know what database programs are available for educational use, and how they compare with each other. That's because as a manager of ICT you may be asked by colleagues to recommend a database program for use in other areas of the curriculum.

Wherever possible, you should seek to get hands-on experience of different software titles. You can do so by:

- talking to your LEA advisors;
- going on INSET courses run by the LEA;
- going on courses run by commercial training providers;
- arranging visits to other schools/colleges in your area (and returning the favour of course!);
- inviting companies in to demonstrate their products, perhaps as part of a training day, and possibly in co-operation with other local schools or colleges;
- taking advantage of 'demo' versions of programs;
- reading reviews in educational computing magazines, computing magazines and newspapers.

Curriculum knowledge

This is the single most important kind of knowledge you will need in order to manage ICT. You cannot possibly do the job properly unless you have in-depth knowledge of what is required to be taught, and how it is to be assessed. To be specific, you need to know at least some of the following:

- what the National Curriculum Programme of Study for IT stipulates;
- the ICT requirements set out in the Programmes of Study of the other curriculum areas;
- the criteria used by OFSTED when evaluating Schools' ICT provision;
- the general findings of OFSTED, as set out in their periodic national and subject reports;
- the reports of other bodies, such as SCAA, the QCA, BECTa and the Examination Boards;
- where appropriate, the ICT requirements of courses such as GNVQ;
- assessment requirements and arrangements laid down by the QCA or other organisations relevant to your school or college;
- other relevant information, such as ICT requirements for trainee teachers;
- current developments in educational ICT.

You can keep abreast of developments by reading the relevant periodicals and by regularly and frequently visiting the official web sites. Also, there are important exhibitions held annually (see Appendix).

You do not need as much knowledge in some of these areas as in others. For example, if you teach in a school, you do not need to know the Initial Teacher Training (ITT) ICT requirements in detail. Equally, you are not expected to memorise the IT Programme of Study. But you must have a good working knowledge of those areas which are relevant to your job, and you must be able to put your hands on the relevant documentation as soon as you require it. (Note that what is regarded as relevant may depend on circumstances. For example, if you take on a trainee teacher, it would be a good idea to know what IT capability s/he is expected to have.)

In this respect, it is imperative to be connected to the internet, personally if needs must, as the Government is making most documents freely available as soon as they are published.

General knowledge

You need two types of general knowledge:

- knowledge of developments in technology;
- knowledge of general educational developments.

Keeping abreast of technological developments is important because as a teacher of IT you must be able to demonstrate that you are aware of what is going on in the world beyond the classroom or the lecture theatre.

There is also a practical reason. Reading about the development of a new or Improved technology could affect your spending plans. For example, when the 56kps modem was announced, you could choose between buying the new 56kps modem straight away, waiting until the price had dropped before buying it, or buying a 33.3kps modem at a new low price. To further complicate matters, there were two different types of 56kps modems, each working on a completely different standard to the other.

In a situation like this, an understanding of the technical issues involved is not absolutely necessary. For those readers old enough to remember, Betamax was commonly regarded as being technically superior to VHS as far as video formats were concerned. However, VHS prevailed as the market leader, and Betamax has disappeared. In that situation, it was more important to know what the market 'thought' than what the 'techies' thought.

It's important to keep up with educational developments in general, because certain changes could affect you in the long run. For example, now that target-setting for schools has been officially implemented, should you not be investigating ways in which computers could be used to cut down on the amount of time staff spend on the associated administration? This may not be a direct part of your job, but getting proactively involved is a good way of promoting ICT – and perhaps even getting yourself promoted! See Chapter 10 for more about using computers to reduce the burden of administration.

The hidden curriculum, or leading by example

People learn by example. They probably learn more from what you do than from what you tell them. In educational terms, this is known as the 'hidden curriculum'.

For example, if you turn up late for every lesson, what message is that giving to the people in your class about your concern for them?

In the context of IT and ICT, setting an example doesn't mean having to build your own computer or write your own program. It means taking care to do the following kinds of things:

- ensure that computers and software are set up and working properly before the lesson;
- observe health and safety regulations and common-sense rules, such as not eating or drinking at the computer;
- observe the correct procedures for using the equipment, such as by shutting down properly rather than simply switching the computer off;
- save your files in folders on the hard disk or on the network with meaningful names, not Doc1, Doc2, or Joan1, Joan2 etc – in fact, you should have a system for naming your files;
- save your work frequently;
- use the correct terminology, and not confuse 'memory', say, with 'hard disk space';
- back up your work regularly;
- produce signs for displays;
- use computers for administrative tasks, such as producing lists of pupils, producing quality worksheets, communicating with other schools, exchanging data with examination boards and so on;
- organise your computer workspace well.

Needless to say, you have to try to ensure that other members of staff, especially those who teach IT, set the same kind of example.

Organisational skills

IT itself is all about systems, so it would be a good idea to reflect this in your daily working practices. This is, perhaps, another example of acknowledging the existence of the hidden curriculum, as mentioned above.

Also, the subject matter is changing rapidly, and curriculum requirements keep changing (although not as frequently as they once did). Both of these facts conspire to produce mountains of paper in the form of Governmental reports, newspaper articles, 'demo' disks and so on.

The only way you can keep on top of it all is by getting organised, and by keeping yourself organised. Therefore, if you are in charge of a budget, invest in low-level technology like filing cabinets and book cases.

Some people get the idea that because they are the manager of ICT, and need to set an example, they must have a paperless office by electronically scanning in all of the documents they will need to refer to. Forget it! You can only contemplate such a solution if you either have a full-time technician or secretary, or have a great deal of non-contact time. In other words, the **totally** paperless office idea is really a non-starter in the average educational establishment.

In any case, there is appropriate and inappropriate ICT. It is not always convenient to read documents on a computer. Also, many people find it easier to read a document in hard copy form than on a screen. As with many other areas of life, you have to strike a balance between different, and to some extent conflicting, objectives.

An important caveat to this is the use of the internet and email. It is becoming increasingly common for schools to be connected to the internet, and so to be able to download files from web sites. Indeed, this is an area in which the DfEE is particularly interested, in order to reduce bureaucracy in schools and colleges (see Chapter 10). Similarly, it is now very easy to exchange views and files through newsgroups and mailing lists.

Once real-time email is in place, colleagues can send each other files by email whether they are in the same office or in a different building altogether. This is almost always faster and more convenient than transferring files by disk or printing them off first.

People skills

There is not much you can do to change your personality, so if after reading this section you decide you're in the wrong job, or were about to enter the wrong job, give this book to a friend and change the direction of your career!

Managing ICT is much more people-oriented than machine-oriented. The days when the ICT manager could get away with writing PASCAL programs in his (they were usually male) spare time and making the computer room as inaccessible as possible are long gone.

These days, a major part of the job is working with colleagues in other subjects to help them to apply ICT in their teaching. In those schools where IT is delivered across the curriculum and not as a discrete subject, this is even more true.

Following on from the need to work with colleagues in this way, you will need to train other staff too. This can be something of a strain where the knowledge of the person you are teaching is much lower than that of any of your pupils! You will also come across people who are frightened of using computers, and those who declare that ICT is not relevant to their subject (and never will be). All these types can present a challenge far worse than any pupils you are likely to have come across!

Paradoxically, you also need to develop the ability to say 'no', because as an ICT manager you will receive requests for a wide range of assistance. See Checklist 2 at the end of this chapter for more information about this.

It is also useful to have report-writing and presentational skills, and perhaps promotional skills. That's because your department will be perceived by everyone as being a bottomless pit into which the lion's share of the available resources are poured. You will frequently be asked to report on progress – in short, to justify the vast expenditure for which you are responsible.

These are just some examples of the sorts of skills you need as far as other people are concerned. For a list of the tasks you will probably be asked to undertake, see Checklist I at the end of this chapter. Taking a more comprehensive view, you will need an ability to:

- be patient;
- listen;
- understand what the other person needs (either personally or for their teaching);
- undertake a needs analysis rather than merely responding to wants;
- make short and long term plans;
- be generally approachable;
- reduce people's trepidation at the thought of using computers;
- be assertive as opposed to aggressive;
- resist the temptation to agree to do everything that people ask you to do, such as formatting disks, changing the printer ribbon, and printing documents for people when they could do it themselves, or be trained to do so – which is more efficient in the long run;
- train without being patronising or sarcastic;
- help people go through a procedure step by step, especially when they're panicking because their computer has crashed;
- train people to the level of skill or self-confidence where they feel they no longer need you;
- communicate well in writing;
- give good presentations (to the senior management team, governors, parents and other staff).

It would be a rare person indeed who could honestly say they have all of these attributes all of the time. But hopefully the list has sketched out the type of person you need to be if you are to do a reasonably good job of managing ICT. If you're a 'techie' who would rather be in a room with a file server than helping someone save their work, then managing ICT in a school or college is not for you.

Checklist 1: Tasks often required of ICT managers

ICT managers are often required to:

- devise and/or implement and/or co-ordinate scheme(s) of work;
- teach IT lessons;
- help other teachers to incorporate ICT in their schemes of work;
- help other teachers to identify opportunities for using ICT;
- identify staff training needs;
- organise and/or run and/or co-ordinate ICT INSET;
- disseminate good practice in the teaching of IT;
- monitor the delivery of IT;
- take responsibility for the reporting of pupils' progress and attainment in IT;
- take responsibility for ensuring that software is properly licensed;
- manage the ICT budget (consumables and other current spending);
- advise the Headteacher or Principal on the purchase of hardware and infrastructure;
- maintain the hardware and other facilities;
- manage technicians;
- manage other teaching staff;
- keep up to date on current developments in computing and telecommunications, and in educational ICT;
- produce the ICT strategy and other documentation, in consultation with the senior management team and other staff;
- ensure that there is a policy in place for accessing the internet (staff as well as pupils);
- act as the contact person with other organisations, such as LEA advisors;

- make presentations to parents, Governors, the senior management team and other teaching staff.

Checklist 2: Favours often requested by other staff

Many of the tasks listed in Checklist 1, plus the following:

- recommend a computer system for personal use;
- format floppy disks;
- recommend software – often highly specialised;
- print certificates;
- fix all hardware problems – computers not booting up, floppy drives not working, etc – immediately;
- fix all software problems – work being saved in the wrong place, or not at all, programs not starting, etc – immediately;
- provide advice to non-teaching staff.

Chapter 2
Managing ICT-specific issues

Introduction

An effective ICT manager often has to take some responsibility for ICT in other subjects as well as his or her own.

For example, if other staff are to use computers effectively in their subjects, they need to have well-maintained computers and the right kind of software. Even if they are in charge of their own budgets as far as ICT is concerned, the ICT manager can still play an important role in disseminating information and helping to reduce wastage of the school's resources.

The main areas in which the ICT manager needs to plan and administer are:

- the delivery and assessment of IT;
- staff training;
- resource evaluation;
- personnel management;
- administration;

- security;
- auditing.

The delivery of IT is covered in Chapters 4 and 6, while the assessment and recording of IT capability is dealt with in Chapter 7. Security and auditing are covered separately in Chapter 3, and staff training is dealt with in Chapter 12.

Evaluating resources

In this section we consider:

- software;
- hardware;
- books and other paper resources.

It could be very advantageous for your institution if it was a rule that all computer-related resources were purchased through you. The potential benefits of this approach include the following:

- because you will be receiving information about new resources coming on to the market, you can advise other staff;
- sometimes the same software can be used in several subject areas, and you are in a position to co-ordinate purchases in order to avoid waste;
- although different people have different preferences in terms of hardware, it makes sense to aim to adopt a particular standard, because the more types of hardware there are, the harder it is to service them all, due to factors like the availability and price of parts, and staff expertise.

If the equipment in each area is regarded as belonging to the institution rather than just that area, you can more easily move equipment around from one area to another as needs change.

In primary schools it is even more important for the school to have a preferred hardware policy, and for the software to be purchased centrally, because usually the ICT Co-ordinator will have a full teaching timetable and no technician.

This raises an important issue: the successful management of ICT relies on taking a wider view than the traditional, somewhat narrow, departmental one usually encountered in secondary schools and colleges.

It makes sense to buy all the hardware, or at least all of the same type of hardware, from one supplier. This gives you 'clout' to negotiate discounts, and also helps you to build up a good relationship. This could lead to benefits such as being able to borrow a computer while one is being repaired, or having useful software thrown in for no charge – but note that if a deal seems too good to be true, it probably is!

Purchasing through your LEA, if possible, is usually a way of getting a bargain without the associated risks. Alternatively, you may be able to purchase the products yourself, but while taking advantage of an LEA-negotiated discount.

Beware of committing yourself to large purchases from small companies that may not be around when you need support. Also, do not fall into the trap of trying to save money by purchasing your hardware from a particular company just because a colleague's nephew works there and can get you a discount.

More information about the financial side of purchasing equipment and software is given in Chapter 9. However, there are two general principles that should guide your decisions:

- whether the product represents good value for money, taking into account factors such as its technical specification, price, technical support and durability;
- whether it uses a standard interface, to facilitate fast learning and transfer of previously-acquired skills.

There are some specific questions you should ask before buying any type of resources. If possible, get a demonstration copy of software, a short-term loan or demonstration of hardware, and samples of printed resources so that you can evaluate them thoroughly before buying them. It is also worth seeking out the views of other schools either locally or through one of the internet newsgroups or mailing lists, your LEA or the subject association to which you belong.

Software evaluation

Ask the questions below, perhaps on a form devised for the purpose.
Ask other staff and, where appropriate, pupils to do the same.

- What is the name of the program?
- What category does it fall into, eg Word Processing, Games?
- Which computer systems will it work on?
- How much is it?
- Where appropriate, how much is a site licence?
- What is the printed documentation like? Will users be able to understand it?
- Is the on-line help good? Will pupils be able to understand it?
- What are the graphics like? For example, do they enhance the program, or distract one's attention?
- What is the colour scheme like? For example, is it too dull, too garish? Will it be difficult for sight-impaired pupils to read?
- Is the layout good? For example, is the screen so cluttered that it is hard to know where to go to next?
- What print options are available?
- How suitable is it for the classes you want it for?
- Does it allow access by people with Special Educational Needs?
- Does it meet the National Curriculum requirements?
- Where appropriate, is it suitable for the examination in question, such as SATs, GCSE, 'A' Level, GNVQ?
- Is it suitable for the scheme of work being followed?
- How easy is it to use? Generally speaking, the more like other programs it is, in terms of doing things like loading, saving and printing files, the faster will pupils (and staff) pick it up.
- Will it attract pupils' interest in the short-term? If you will have to motivate them to use the program, perhaps that would not be an effective use of your time.
- Does it make good use of the computer?
- Will it be able to maintain pupils' interest in the long-term, eg through differentiated and/or open-ended tasks? If not, it still could be quite handy to have it on the system so that pupils can work through it either as a break from their other work or during the last five minutes of the lesson.

- Is it good value for money? To some extent your answer to this is dependent upon your answers to all of the previous questions, but there are over-riding factors too, particularly concerning price. For example, the software may be excellent in every regard, but the cost of a site licence may be prohibitive. Or it may be affordable, but be no more effective than an alternative resource, such as another program or a book. Sometimes the price may seem high, but technical support may be free, or there may be free upgrades for a year or longer. In other words, don't judge value for money by price alone.
- Will it enhance your existing software resources?

Note that most of these questions apply even to free software, because of the opportunity costs involved.

Hardware evaluation

There are many different kinds of hardware, and so you will need different criteria for each type. For example, you will obviously need to be looking at different things when deciding which printer to buy than when deciding which computer system to buy.

Before purchasing any piece of hardware, you should find out what to look for. The commercial computer magazines often carry comparative reviews of products. These are useful not only for the information on particular products, but also for seeing the criteria used to evaluate them. There are also web sites which are useful in this context.

Regardless of the particular kind of hardware, there are some general questions you can attempt to answer:

- Is it easy to set up, both physically and in terms of any installation software required?
- Is it easy for non-experts to use?
- Is it robust? For example, will it be able to cope with lots of different kinds of task each and every day?
- Is it easy to maintain? For example, if a printer, how easy is it to change the toner or ink cartridge? Are parts readily available?
- Is it costly to maintain? Sometimes a high initial expenditure can be justified by low maintenance costs – but only if you are likely

to keep it for long enough for it to pay for itself. As an example, an inkjet printer is cheap to buy but expensive to run, whereas a laser printer is expensive to buy but cheap to run.

- Is it recommended in (educational) magazine reviews?
- Is it compatible with existing systems?
- How new is the technology it uses? The newer the technology, the higher the price, and the more undiscovered bugs there are, generally speaking. Are you prepared to wait for a few months, or to buy older technology at a reduced price?
- Is it good value for money?
- What technical support is provided? (See Chapter 9.)

Books and other paper resources evaluation

IT is not just about using computers, and it is useful to have teaching resources such as books from which you can set work. Unfortunately, IT is still very much in its infancy in this context, compared with other subjects such as Maths, Science and English. Nevertheless, there are books out there, and there seem to be more and more titles coming out all the time.

Obtain inspection copies where possible, and ask other IT teachers what they think of the books or resources you are interested in purchasing. A good place to canvas opinions is in one of the internet news groups given in the Appendix.

The types of questions to ask are:

- Will users be able to understand it?
- What is the layout like? Books which look like teen magazines tend to be visually distracting.
- Is it accurate? Obviously, unless the book is meant to be for undergraduates, some licence may be OK, but you still have to be careful. For example, are the diagrams correctly labelled?
- Does it meet the National Curriculum requirements?
- Where appropriate, is it suitable for the examination in question, such as SATs, GCSE, 'A' Level, GNVQ?
- Is it suitable for the scheme of work being followed?
- How easy is it to use for finding information?

- Is it interesting?
- Is it challenging?
- Does it have non-computer based exercises?
- Are the tasks realistic for the people in your class?
- Is it good value for money? It may be cheaper in the long run to buy sets of photocopiable resources than sets of textbooks.

Personnel management

There are five kinds of staff you may need to manage:

- teaching staff for whom you are directly responsible, such as those in your department if you work in a secondary school or college;
- teaching staff for whom you are not directly responsible;
- technicians, secretaries, cleaners and caretakers;
- senior management;
- 'outsiders', such as advisors and sales people.

Teaching staff for whom you are directly responsible

This is not relevant in most schools, such as in primary schools in which all teachers teach IT to their classes, and the ICT manager only co-ordinates. In many secondary schools the ICT manager has two or three staff who each teach only one or two hours of IT a week.

It is unreasonable, and unrealistic, to expect teachers who spend most of their week teaching a different subject to devote the same amount of time preparing IT lessons. However, you still have every right to expect staff to be:

- well-prepared;
- well-informed about the subject and competent in the use of ICT;
- up-to-date with their marking and other administration.

There are several ways by which you can attempt to achieve this happy state of affairs, including the following:

- cut down on lesson preparation time by adopting a Unit-based approach (see Chapter 6.);
- use ICT to ease teachers' administrative burden (see Chapter 10);
- encourage staff to share any worksheets they produce, as this reduces everyone else's burden; these materials should be available electronically so that other staff may adapt them easily and quickly – it should also go without saying that staff will only continue to share their ideas if you acknowledge them);
- prepare a list of tasks to be done by each group in the event of a teacher's absence, so that staff can tick off work as it is completed by each group (see Figure 2.1);
- homework may also be set for and by all staff who teach IT;
- hold meetings once a fortnight rather than once a week – if you *have* to have a meeting once a week, make one of them an INSET session (see Chapter 12).

In return for your efforts to reduce the amount of time spent by your staff on routine tasks, you have the right to expect them to attend relevant INSET and ensure that their lesson preparation, marking and record-keeping are up to date.

In the long run, you should try to persuade your Head or Principal to allow you to have a smaller rather than a larger team, so that each person is teaching more IT, making it more worthwhile for them to put the effort in.

If you are allowed a choice in who teaches IT, experience shows that you are better off with an enthusiastic teacher who requires training than someone who thinks they are a computer expert. Most of the time those who fall into the latter category also believe that they are IT experts, which is **not** the same thing (see the Preface for a definition of IT).

Please tick off each group as it completes the work.							
Cover Work	**Number**	**7–1**	**7–2**	**7–3**	**7–4**	**7–5**	**7–6**
Use Paintbrush to explore all the different tools. Make notes on what each one does.	1						
Use Micrografx draw to explore all the different tools. Make notes on what each one does.	2						
Use Paintbrush to draw a picture. Then use Word to write a story, and include your picture in it. Use either Copy and Paste or the Insert Picture command.	3						
Open the Accessories window on the desktop. Make notes on what each proram does, using Word.	4						
What are the main differences between Word and WordPad? Make notes using Word	5						

Instructions to IT staff:

1 Stick your copy of this to the desk.

2 Leave instructions as to which

Instructions to cover teacher:

1 Please tell pupils what work to do, if it is not written on board.

2 Tick the sheet to show what work was set for this group.

Thank you.

Figure 2.1 - *IT department cover work*

(Note that this has been completed with a Year 7 course in mind, but the general idea is valid for any Year group.)

Teaching staff for whom you are not directly responsible

Managing staff for whom you are not directly responsible is harder than managing your own staff, because you are not their line manager – or are you?

In a secondary school, if IT is to be delivered entirely through other subjects, you have the same responsibilities as Head of Department as you would if the subject were being delivered discretely.

You must keep in mind that, as far as IT is concerned, you are their line manager. If, for example, the Maths Department has agreed to undertake to teach modelling through spreadsheets, they have an obligation to follow your scheme of work, to make sure their lessons are prepared, to mark work and to keep their records in order. It is your right – and duty – to insist on these.

In a primary school setting, similar considerations apply. The ICT manager will need to make sure staff know what the scheme of work is (and perhaps even help to create it) and how they can deliver it.

To be able to discharge some of your duties, you will need to hold meetings. You have equal rights in this regard as other managers. You may need to negotiate times with the other subject managers, but you should negotiate on an equal footing. In primary schools, where Heads of Department do not exist as such, you will still need to call meetings, probably in co-operation with the Deputy Head or Headteacher and Year or phase co-ordinators.

Where staff in other subjects are having to use computers to enhance the work they do, you may need to ensure that they have a basic understanding of how to conduct a lesson which makes use of computers.

Offer to make available to other staff any useful bits and pieces you've developed, such as templates, worksheets and so on.

Many schools and colleges have an ICT Committee to look at policy and spending issues. If you are Chair of such a group, you need to be clear about its purpose and its status. This subject is discussed in more detail in Chapter 6.

As far as management of committees is concerned, all the usual rules apply. For example you should ensure that:

- there is an Agenda well in advance of a meeting;
- Minutes are circulated as soon as possible after the meeting;
- everyone has the opportunity to speak if they want to;
- there are no personal attacks on people for their views;
- the Agenda is adhered to;
- the meeting finishes on time.

Technicians, secretaries, cleaners and caretakers

It is unusual for primary schools, and even many secondary schools, to enjoy the services of a technician. Although it is possible to get by without one, a list of the tasks required to be done (see Chapter 5) indicates that technicians are a necessity rather than a luxury.

In addition to asking your technician to carry out the tasks outlined in Chapter 5, you may also be able to ask for his/her opinion on technical matters.

Often, technicians have more of a grasp of the nitty-gritty of particular hardware, and this can be both an advantage and a disadvantage.

You can ask your technician to investigate the merits and demerits of competing hardware, such as servers or cabling. However, you need to make it clear that you will take the final decision – which will be based on wider considerations than technical ones.

It is important that technicians be kept aware of your wider aims. This means that you should ask them to attend ICT meetings now and again (although this may not be possible due to the hours they are contracted to work).

Technicians should be given the opportunity to develop and improve their skills, despite the risk represented by their consequently improved marketability.

Technicians should be provided with opportunities to meet other technicians from neighbouring schools and colleges, in order to discuss common problems. It is quite often the case that someone has found a solution to a problem you've been experiencing. It should also be possible to exchange ideas via the internet or an LEA intranet.

As far as technicians, secretaries, cleaners and caretakers are concerned, you should:

■ treat them with respect;
■ keep them informed.

These are also good rules to apply when dealing with anybody, but the reason they are mentioned here is that all too often teachers fail to apply them when dealing with ancillary staff.

Senior management

To some extent all staff have to 'manage' their senior management team, or members of it. However, this is especially important for anyone who typically spends vast sums of money. Managing the senior management team (SMT) becomes even more crucial if you must deliver the IT curriculum through other subjects, because you may need their co-operation even more in order to make the system work.

You need to 'manage' the SMT in order to ensure that funds are available in the right amounts and in the right way (see Chapter 9), to obtain the rooms you require and to help get the teaching team you need. Also, research has shown that if members of the SMT have a positive attitude towards ICT, and are seen to make use of ICT in their teaching and administrative tasks, other teaching staff are more favourably disposed towards it.

Here are some suggested ways of influencing the SMT:

■ Maintain a high profile. This means, for example, making sure that any documentation you produce is done with a computer, and to the highest standard (see Chapter 11).

- Keep statistics on the use of the computers (see the section on auditing in Chapter 3). This is useful not only to help you decide on spending plans, but also to show (hopefully) increasing use of the system, and *better* use of it.

- If subject managers are asked to contribute voluntarily to reports to Governors, volunteer. Remember that it is usually the Governors, ultimately, who decide on large-scale investment plans in ICT. Your report should include examination successes and improvements if appropriate (this applies to reports to the SMT as well).

- When OFSTED (and other) reports come out about the delivery of IT nationally, summarise the results for the staff who teach IT, and ask the SMT if it would like copies. Relate such reports to the experience in your institution, as appropriate.

- Offer to make all such reports available on disk, so that people can view them on their own computers.

- Offer to address the SMT on the development of IT and ICT in the school or college.

- Ask to be included on the SMT, because decisions about ICT affect everyone else, if only because of the sums of money involved.

- If you are not to be included in the SMT, ask to be represented on the team by an existing (and preferably sympathetic and knowledgeable) member.

Administration

The ICT Handbook

Even if you do not **have** to produce a handbook, you should do so. The purpose of the handbook is to inform staff, especially new staff, what your procedures and expectations are. If you are inspected, this handbook will provide evidence that you have attempted to develop pertinent policies, procedures and systems.

The quality of the handbook should not be judged by its weight. It should be useful, which means it must be accessible, not like an encyclopaedia. The items it may contain are:

- a statement about the role of ICT in everyday life and in the school or college;
- the ICT policy (see p. 26);
- the staff who teach IT (perhaps as an appendix or as a separate document, to allow for changes from year to year);
- a guide to the terminology used – so that all IT teachers use the same terminology, and so that others know what you are all talking about;
- the scheme of work you are following, with details of what is covered in each year, broken down into Units if appropriate, and including a (brief) statement about the philosophy underlying the course, and its aims and learning objectives;
- general details about the examination courses you are following (if any), such as coursework requirements, and information about where further details may be found;
- general guidance on assessment; planning requirements, including lesson planning, cover work, homework and record-keeping – if possible, including examples of pro formas you would like staff to use;
- details of the records to be kept, and where the blank sheets (if applicable) are stored – staff should not have to chase after you for forms to fill in;
- a summary of the relevant Key Stages of the National Curriculum IT Order – many people can never find the document when they need it, so including a summary in your handbook can be really helpful;
- **all** the procedures, eg how to book the equipment and even how to start the computers up: new staff do not know what to do, and they do not know what they don't know, and so will not necessarily ask the right questions;
- a guide to the facilities, including statements like 'If you have a large group, ie more than 20, use room X, otherwise use room Y', where applicable;
- INSET offered;
- the times the computer facilities are available;
- how to report hardware and software faults.

Ideally, the handbook should be no more than 20 or so pages, with double-spaced typing, and with a table of contents.

The ICT policy

The ICT policy sets out the general parameters within which you and your institution works. A typical policy will consist of the headings below, most of which are dealt with elsewhere in this book:

- Statement of intent. This states the institution's general aims, such as 'All pupils will be IT-literate by the time they leave', or 'All pupils will develop competence and confidence in using ICT'.
- Equal opportunities.
- How the IT curriculum is delivered.
- How IT capability is assessed.
- How pupil achievement is monitored and recorded.
- Hardware purchasing policy.
- Software purchasing policy.
- System maintenance. If you have a policy of, say, deleting files that have not been accessed for a particular period of time, include this in your Policy.
- INSET policy.
- The basis for replacing equipment. For example, there may be a rolling 5 year investment programme.
- The role of the ICT Committee if there is one (see Chapter 6).
- Software copyright.
- Antivirus policy.
- Data protection.
- Internet access policy (referring to the acceptable use policy, if there is one). This is a contract through which pupils agree to not attempt to access certain kinds of web site, and accepting responsibility if they are found to be doing so. See Chapter 13 also.
- How ICT in the school or college is monitored.
- How the ICT Policy itself is monitored.

Like the Handbook, the ICT Policy should not be bulky. In fact, it should be no more than five or six pages long.

The ICT Strategy

Many ICT managers have found it useful to have separate documents setting out general matters which do not change from year to year, such as the school's method of delivering the IT curriculum and its stance on software copyright, and aspects which can and do change from year to year, such as the current ICT INSET programme. The former is sometimes referred to as the ICT Policy, and the latter as the ICT Strategy.

Whatever you call it, the Strategy should be no longer than a couple of sides of A4 and give the reader a good idea of what you will be spending and doing in the coming period (from the next financial year to up to 5 years' time), and how that spending will enable the aims of the curriculum to be realised.

Chapter 3

Managing the hardware and software

Introduction

Managing ICT involves more than organising equipment booking or staff INSET. You also have to consider such matters as copyright issues and theft prevention.

This chapter deals with two broad areas:

- security;
- auditing.

Security

Under the heading 'security' we consider the following:

- copyright issues;
- antivirus measures;
- backing up your data;

- theft prevention;
- responding to a break-in;
- preventing user access.

As you can see from this list, the term 'security' is used here in its widest sense – to mean security from criminal prosecution as much as anything else. Remember – ignorance is no excuse in the eyes of the law.

Make sure that ICT policies on issues such as copyright and virus checking are accessible and unequivocal. This can be done with posters such as the one shown in Figure 3.1.

The School's Policy on...

Software Copyright

✓ **We use only legally-purchased software.**
✓ **Any unauthorised programs found on out computers are deleted without warning.**
✓ **Our computers are not used for making illegal copies of software.**
✓ **Shareware and similar programs are only used in accordance with the licence agreement supplied with the program.**
✓ **If you need advice about software licences, see [insert name of ICT manager].**

Figure 3.1 – Example of a policy poster

Make sure that original program disks and CDs, antivirus software and software licences and related documentation are locked away.

Copyright of printed materials

Books, newspapers, magazines and even the National Curriculum are all protected by copyright.

Before making copies, and especially before making multiple copies or electronic copies of printed material (by scanning, say), find out what you can and cannot do. Your reprographics officer or school or college secretary should be able to tell you how many copies you can make, since this will partly depend on how many 'credits' remain on your institution's licence.

The material itself will usually carry an indication too. For example, it may say that you can make copies for educational use as long as you acknowledge the source.

Copyright of web pages

These are also copyright. The copyright belongs to the author or the organisation for whom the pages have been created. It is commonly thought that it is OK to use other people's web materials on your own web pages as long as you acknowledge the source. This is not the case, unless there is a statement saying so. (If in doubt, email the author.) Shoplifting does not suddenly cease to be an offence if you tell everyone the name of the shop.

Copyright of software

There is always some debate as to whether software can be copied for some purposes even without explicit permission, such as in order to make a backup. There are also different kinds of licences, such as site licences, network licences and individual licences. Moreover, some site licences allow teachers to have a copy of the software for use at home, whereas others don't.

It is better to err on the side of caution, and assume that you cannot make a copy of the software unless you have explicit written permission to do so. You should get written permission even if the company that publishes the software tells you over the phone that it's OK for you to copy it. That's because if you are ever prosecuted for software theft, the plaintiff (ie the person or organisation bringing the charge) could well be the Federation Against Software Theft (FAST) rather than the company with which you've been dealing.

Antivirus measures

Data can be irretrievably lost through the actions of viruses. Virus protection is therefore necessary, and potentially expensive. It can be expensive because you normally have to have one licence per computer, and you have to take out a subscription to keep the software up to date rather than pay a one-off cost. Not having antivirus software can work out much more expensive in the long run. If you work in a large institution, it is worth trying to negotiate a substantial discount. Note that your LEA may provide antivirus software at low or no cost.

A kind of antivirus policy is to ban people from taking disks away and bringing their own ones in. This is both difficult, if not impossible, to enforce, and runs counter to another objective, that of encouraging other staff to use the computer system as much as possible. It is, in any case, incomplete, since viruses can be transmitted by email attachments and CDs.

Backups

It is essential to back up data every day. A backup can mean not only the difference between pupils retrieving their work and having to do it again, but even between getting the network up and running again within minutes and having to arrange a call-out.

If you have a network installed, backing up is very easy. Set the automatic backup scheduler on the server to make a backup every night at, say, 1 am. All you have to do is make sure that somebody (you or your technician) puts the right tape in before you leave each day. Ideally, you should adopt a strategy such as:

- have two weeks' worth of tapes, plus one extra, ie 11 tapes;
- mark each one for week 1 as 1/Monday, 1/Tuesday etc;
- mark each one for week 2 as 2/Monday, 2/Tuesday etc;

- after the initial backup, set it up to backup only the changes made;
- at the end of each term, do a full backup again on the extra tape;
- keep a log of the backups you have made.

This is one feasible approach, but your local adviser or supplier may recommend alternatives.

In addition, you should have the following:

- a spare tape, in case one of the others breaks;
- the tape supplied with the server (hopefully), containing all of the server software;
- a cleaning tape, for cleaning the tape backup device once a week.

If you have a large number of stand-alones then making backups for all of them becomes impossible. You must therefore:

- lock down each computer to prevent unauthorised access (see below);
- place more responsibility on individual users to back up their own work;
- place the original program disks and CDs under lock and key so that you can reinstall them if necessary (you should do this anyway, to prevent theft);
- make a note of, or print out, specific software settings so that you can re-create your set up as quickly as possible should you need to;
- instead of, or in addition to, the previous recommendation, create a CD-ROM from which you can set up all of the computers identically – if, of course, you have a CD-Writer.

Theft prevention

As with other parts of this book, this section is not intended to be a definitive guide. Before doing anything you should:

- make sure that your inventory is up-to-date – see the section on stock-checking in Chapter 5;
- find out your school's or college's policy in this area, such as whether there is a rule that every new item of equipment has to be security marked in a particular way;

- discuss security with the caretaker or site supervisor;
- if relevant, find out if the LEA has a recommended policy;
- with permission from the Head or Principal, seek the advice of the LEA security officer or the local police force's crime prevention unit.

There are a number of physical measures you can take to prevent theft of equipment. For example, you can:

- bolt all computers and printers to the work tops;
- secure equipment with cables, which is usually less costly and time-consuming than bolting everything down, but possibly not quite as effective in acting as a deterrent or slowing a thief down;
- install alarms, either on each item or in the rooms as a whole – this is obviously a much more expensive option;
- secure all mice and keyboards with cable ties, making it harder for someone to steal them quickly, such as at the end of a lesson;
- mouse balls can be expensive to replace, especially en masse, so either glue the mouse ball 'door' (which makes mouse cleaning hard) or remove the mouse ball after use (which can be done quite easily by teachers in charge of rooms where there are only one or two computers) and pupils should be taught to respect the equipment, and there should be proper procedures for starting and finishing lessons using the computer (see Chapter 5);
- security mark each item with a special marker whose writing only shows up under ultra-violet light – the usual recommendation is to write the school or college postcode;
- write the school or college postcode, and other details such as the computer's number, on the equipment with an indelible spirit marker;
- as a variation of the previous suggestion, deface the equipment – this involves making the equipment virtually completely unsaleable, such as by writing or engraving the institution's name in a prominent place (or by asking art students to paint or stencil on the equipment);
- make sure doors and windows are kept locked, particularly in out-of-the-way offices, and especially in places where there is easy access to the street or car park;

■ erect notices to the effect that all equipment is security marked.

Many of these approaches are not mutually exclusive. For example, you could bolt the equipment down, mark it with a special marker and mark it with a spirit marker.

As is always the case, you will not stop a determined thief. You can, however, make it as hard as possible for people to steal the equipment in the first place, and then to sell it on. Also, the measures outlined above will certainly do much to help prevent opportunist theft.

If equipment is distributed around the school or college, all teachers should follow the same security guidelines.

Find out if you are expected to pay for security measures out of your capitation. There is a case for saying it is a whole school or policy matter, especially if computers are distributed around the site.

Responding to a break-in

If the worst happens and you suffer a break-in and theft of computer equipment, you will need to carry out a certain procedure. What this exact procedure is will depend on your school or college – find out from the caretaker or the secretary what you are supposed to do, and make sure other staff know as well.

Generally speaking, the procedure will be something like this:

1   Do not touch anything, especially door and window handles, in case the police want to dust for fingerprints.

2   Put a notice up telling others not to touch anything.

3   Call the caretaker, or the secretary, who will call the police, or call the police yourself if there is nobody else available.

4   Make a list of the equipment stolen. For each item, note the type of equipment, name of the model, distinguishing marks (such as the postcode engraved on it) and serial number (which should be recorded in your stock book).

5   Make a note of the date and time of the theft, or when you discovered it.

6 Obtain a crime reference number from the police, possibly via the caretaker.

7 Inform the Head or Principal.

8 Put in an insurance claim.

Note the following points about claiming on your insurance:

■ insurance policies typically cover break-ins, not walk-in thefts – but it may be worth putting a claim in anyway;

■ your insurance policy will probably include a clause about claiming within a certain period of time, such as within 2 working weeks of the theft;

■ when claiming, bear in mind that you should be looking to replace equipment for the same purpose, not necessarily at the same value. For example, you may have been using an old computer for computer control activities. That model of computer may not be worth very much, and may even be no longer available. If the only way you can replace it is by purchasing a more modern computer with a higher value, your insurance policy ought to be able to allow you to do so. Clearly, this is something you will want to check out **before** you actually need to know.

Preventing user access

Time can very easily be wasted by people changing settings, installing software, deleting software and so on. You not only waste time trying to rectify the problem, but in the meantime others may not be able to use the affected computers. You should take steps to prevent the kinds of access listed below.

■ *Access to the BIOS.* You can gain access to a PC's basic set-up, and thereby easily prevent it working at all, by a key as it is booting up. You should therefore set your own password for access to the BIOS on each PC. At the very least you should disable the message which tells the user what key to press to gain access to the BIOS.

■ *Access to system files.* You only need to make one or two small alterations to certain files in order to cause mayhem. Either disable access to the system files, or buy a utility that will do so for you. (There are shareware programs available on the internet that you can try out before buying – see the Appendix for details of where to find them.) If you have a network, it is worth buying network management software that will do all the work for you.

■ *Access to the desktop configuration.* Ideally, each computer's desktop should either look the same every time anyone boots it up, or look the same whenever anyone in a certain group uses it. In other words, it should not be possible for any unauthorised person to change, add or delete anything on the desktop. You can buy software which prevents this kind of access for both networks and stand-alones.

■ *Access to software installation and uninstallation.* It should not be possible for unauthorised people to install or delete software. If possible, make sure you have what is called an 'image' of each computer's configuration, so that in the event of a mishap you can quickly restore it to what it was before. There are utilities to do this for stand-alones, and some network solutions have this facility as part of their feature set. Alternatively, create a CD-ROM from which you can set up all of the computers identically.

■ *Access from outside the organisation.* This is prevented through the installation of a firewall. There are different kinds of firewall, and the technicalities involved are beyond the scope of this book. Consult a telecommunications expert, or seek the advice of your LEA if this is appropriate.

Auditing

It is useful to audit the use of computer equipment and software in order to be able to:

■ plan future expenditure;

■ target particular areas of the school or college, either in terms of physical areas or Departments;

■ justify recent expenditure if you are required to do so;

■ write reports for the senior management team and the governing body;

■ investigate an individual pupil's progress;

■ check what individual pupils have been accessing – this could be useful in the event of a dispute about the pupil's progress.

If you cannot find suitable auditing software for stand-alones (many network solutions come with built-in auditing software), establish a manual system. This could involve asking people to note down what software they used, and why, over a certain period of time in a particular room, but clearly any manual method is not as reliable as an automated one on the whole.

Built-in auditing software should enable you to keep track of the activities listed below.

- *Equipment usage.* This will help you to decide whether, say, you need another printer in a particular room, or more computers there.

- *Software usage.* It is useful to know how much use is being made of different programs, because that knowledge can help you decide whether or not to upgrade them, or buy licence extensions for them.

- *Room usage.* If one room is being used appreciably more than another one, it would be useful to try to analyse why.

- *Pupil usage.* It can be very useful to be able to track what software was used by a particular pupil and when, especially where there is a difference of opinion between parents and teachers regarding the quantity of work done over the period in question. (Note, however, that false results are given if, say, a pupil leaves the computer logged on during play-time.)

Not everything can be audited automatically. Other useful information you may want to obtain from time to time includes the following items:

- *Other Heads of Departments' plans* for using ICT over the next year or more.

- *Staff computer and IT skills.* An annual audit would help you to devise a suitable INSET program for the academic year.

- *Pupils' IT skills.* This knowledge is useful both for helping you to judge how well IT is being delivered and for informing staff about what the pupils can do – this can often make the difference between someone using computers in their lessons and their not doing so.

Note that if IT is delivered in a cross-curricular way, this auditing is both necessary and, usually, difficult – see Chapter 4 for further details.

■ *Home computers.* Knowing whether pupils have access to computers at home has been held to be useful. Perhaps it is, from an academic point of view. In practice, access to a computer at home does not mean knowing how to use a computer effectively. In any case, as long as there is one student who doesn't have access to a computer at home, it is unfair to set homework that relies on computer access – unless you are willing and able to provide such access outside teaching hours, and the student is able and willing to take advantage of its availability.

Chapter 4
Managing computers in classrooms

Modes of delivery

Introduction

There are three main ways of delivering the IT Curriculum:

- discrete delivery;
- cross-curricular teaching;
- a combination of the previous two approaches.

We now consider the management implications of each.

Discrete delivery

This is where IT is delivered in a timetabled slot, in the same way as any other subject. The rationale behind doing this is that IT consists of concepts and knowledge that have to be taught, and which would not necessarily be learnt by pupils simply by using computers.

In other words, this approach recognises that IT is not just about using computers, but about knowing when and how to use computers to their best advantage. More and more primary schools too now timetable IT lessons in computer rooms, although this is difficult given the demands of the Literacy and Numeracy Strategies.

Ideally, the subject IT should be:

■ taught by staff who understand IT as a thinking process, not simply people who know how to use some software application – according to OFSTED, 'The poor subject knowledge of teachers continues to be closely linked with unsatisfactory teaching.' (OFSTED, 'The Annual Report of Her Majesty's Chief Inspector of Schools, Standards and Quality in Education', 1997–98, paragraph 44);

■ timetabled for at least 1 hour per week throughout the year. In secondary schools, circus arrangements, in which classes are taught for, say, 2 hours per week for half the year rather than 1 hour per week for the whole year, are not as effective because pupils have a long time in which to forget what they've learnt. Indeed, if pupils are taught IT in the first half of Year 7, and then again in the second half of Year 8, they will have a whole year (potentially) in which to lose the skills and knowledge they have acquired;

■ taught in all years at school.

From the point of view of managing the delivery of the IT Programme of Study, this approach has several **advantages**. For example, it is easier to ensure that:

■ pupils are taught the same concepts, in a systematic way, rather than by accident or haphazardly;

■ the IT National Curriculum Programme of Study is covered in its entirety, especially at Key Stage 4;

■ the higher order skills in the National Curriculum IT order are addressed.

However, the potential **disadvantages** of discrete delivery of IT include the considerations that:

■ it may be difficult to find the resources to enable pupils to apply their IT skills to other areas of the curriculum;

- teachers of other subjects may think they don't have to do anything with computers because it's all being done in the timetabled slot.

To overcome the disadvantages of the discrete delivery approach, you will need to employ your 'people skills' to the fullest, in order to persuade:

- the senior management team that adequate computer resources be made available;
- other staff to incorporate ICT in their schemes of work. It is likely that the next verstion of the National Curriculum will be much more specific than the present one in terms of the IT skills that pupils are expected to use in subjects other than IT. Nevertheless, your persuasion skills may still be necessary in order to ensure that IT is used in other lessons.

Cross-curricular delivery

This is where IT is delivered in the periods allocated to other parts of the curriculum. There are several different interpretations of what 'cross-curricular' means:

- in secondary schools and colleges, various departments undertake to teach certain aspects of IT through their own subjects; for example, the mathematics department may teach spreadsheets;
- again in secondary schools and colleges, the IT department 'borrows' time from departments; for example, it may use 6 periods from geography in the first half-term, 6 from English in the second half-term and so on; often, the subject teacher is asked to provide a suitable context for the IT lessons, and is present in the lesson, quite often for INSET purposes;
- IT is used as a normal aspect of lessons in different subjects. This is the approach often adopted by primary schools;
- sometimes, IT is not taught at all as such, but is used as a tool in other subjects.

The **advantages** of the cross-curricular approach from a management perspective include the following:

- it may reduce the need to have computer rooms, which are expensive in terms of room space;

- pupils are shown automatically how IT can be applied in a practical context, potentially getting around the need to construct artificial examples;

- it 'forces' subject staff to learn how to use IT in order to apply it in their lessons, so in theory at least you do not have to persuade lots of people to grasp the nettle;

- it ensures that the ICT resources are used across the board, making it easier to justify further expenditure on equipment and software.

The **disadvantages** of the cross-curricular approach in terms of management include the following:

- large numbers of staff may need to be trained in IT and its application in the classroom;

- it is potentially more difficult to ensure that there is not an emphasis on software skills at the expense of problem-solving skills, and on low-level concepts at the expense of higher level concepts;

- similarly, it may be difficult, if not impossible, to ensure that the IT Programme of Study is covered, and that the quality of its delivery is consistent across the board, and to monitor what skills are being learnt by the pupils;

- where time is 'borrowed' from other Departments, this can create resentment in subject staff who would rather be teaching their own subject;

- IT may be perceived as the poor cousin of the curriculum. This can have a deleterious effect on pupils' decisions to take it further (see Chapter 11, on promoting ICT).

A combination of the previous two approaches

This is where pupils are taught IT as a subject, **and** are given opportunities to apply it.

This approach can combine the best of the discrete and cross-curricular methods, and avoid the worst aspects of them. It is cited again and again, for example in reports from OFSTED, as yielding the best results.

For example:

In order to promote progression, IT teaching needs to be backed up with curricular opportunities to apply the skills that have been learned.'

(OFSTED, 1996)

Greater success in IT was associated with a good mix of timetabled IT lessons, treating the subject effectively in its own right, together with a significant application of IT in other subjects.

(Goldstein, 1997)

From a management perspective this approach makes planning easy. For example, you can tell other subject managers what you will be covering and when, so that they can use ICT at an appropriate time. For example, it makes sense for LOGO to be used in maths after the pupils have been taught how to use it in their IT lessons, because then the maths teachers do not have to worry about teaching it, and can focus instead on its applications.

Also, staff are more likely to use ICT in their lessons if they feel confident that the pupils know what they are doing. You can facilitate this by issuing periodic bulletins informing staff what IT has recently been covered by various year groups.

Distribution of resources: advantages and disadvantages of each type

The nature of the curriculum will clearly have an effect on the distribution of computer resources around the building. Put simply, to teach IT as a discrete subject efficiently, you need computer rooms, while to embed IT across the curriculum effectively you need classroom access on demand.

Types of computer distribution

There are 3 main types of arrangement:

- computer rooms;
- single/small number of computers in classrooms;

■ clusters of computers around the school or college.

Advantages and disadvantages of these distribution types

The main **advantages** of computer rooms are that it is easier to:

■ teach concepts to whole classes at once;

■ ensure that pupils have access to computers in IT lessons;

■ manage the equipment;

■ keep the equipment secure;

■ oversee health and safety matters;

■ share equipment like printers and scanners.

The main **disadvantages** are:

■ they can encourage a 'techie' approach to the subject;

■ they can give the impression that IT is a separate activity which does not occur in other areas of the curriculum;

■ there may not be enough room to do work away from the computer;

■ it can be difficult for other classes to gain access to computers.

The **advantages** of a single or small number of computers in classrooms are:

■ pupils can use the computer when they need to, as part of their work, rather than as an artificial activity;

■ the arrangement reinforces the idea that IT is naturally a part of other activity;

■ used properly, a single computer can be used to provide remedial learning, or as a resource for research and group work.

The **disadvantages** are:

■ security is harder to maintain;

■ good practice may be harder to reinforce;

■ it is more difficult to teach concepts to a whole class at once (because it will take time for everyone in the class to try out what they've been shown).

The **advantages** of cluster (including 'café') arrangements are:

- they provide a flexible, non-bookable resource which can be used as required;
- they provide areas where pupils can work, perhaps in a less formal setting;
- they reinforce the view that computers are an integral part of our daily lives.

The **disadvantages** of clusters include the following:

- maintenance and security of equipment may be quite difficult;
- they cannot easily be used for group or class work.

Managing computer rooms

Introduction

(Note that similar considerations apply to the management of one to four computers in classrooms and the management of clusters of computers.)

Computer rooms are different from the rooms in the rest of the school or college for one simple reason (apart from the obvious): other staff not only use them, but also use the equipment in them. No other department has this situation. Yes, other staff may occasionally have to take a class into a science laboratory because of room changes, but they will not get the test tubes and Bunsen burners out!

With this in mind, you must answer these questions:

- How can the potential damage to equipment be minimised?
- How can inconvenience to others (arising from, say, poor printing practices) be minimised?
- How can you make sure that the experience of both staff and pupils is a positive one?

Some of the answers to these questions lie outside the computer room itself. For example, you might ask staff to attend a short induction course on the subject of class management in a computer room before they take a class into a computer room.

Useful displays

It is amazing how many computer rooms are festooned with posters which are attractive but useless. Posters should not be put up merely to make a room look attractive. They should serve a useful purpose, and make your management role easier. Examples of useful posters include:

- rules of behaviour;
- simple instructions, such as 'Save your work every 10 minutes';
- software guides.

When creating posters, bear in mind that they should be readable from all over the room. As a rule, letters should be at least half an inch high for every 15 feet.

A useful approach is to create a poster for each of the main programs used, with each poster containing the information required to be able to carry out basic functions like saving and printing.

A good question to keep in the forefront of your mind is: could a complete novice come into this room and get some useful work done by following my posters?

Using humour often gets the point across effectively.

Instructions should be expressed positively rather than negatively as far as possible. For example, 'Walk into the room quietly' is usually more effective than 'Don't enter the room noisily'.

It is also useful to display examples of pupils' work. Not only does this enhance the self-esteem of the pupils themselves, it also serves to show others what work goes on using computers. Also, a nice display helps to maintain high standards of behaviour by underlining the importance of the appearance of the room.

Manuals for staff and pupils

Taking the view that a complete novice should be able to use the facilities to advantage, you should consider writing a manual for pupils to use, and one for staff to use. The pupils' manual should be available for each computer, while staff should be given their own, or there should be one per room or Department. These manuals should contain:

- instructions on how to start and finish;
- where files may be saved (eg where floppy disks may be obtained);
- a glossary of terms, such as 'click' and double-click;
- information about printing, such as where the printer is located, credits required and so on;
- where to obtain more help, from manuals and the like;
- how to obtain assistance from another person;
- a simple guide to each program: how to start and finish, and how to create, save, open and print a file.

In addition to these points, the staff version should also contain:

- instructions on how to make work available for pupils;
- pointers on how to look after the facilities, how to minimise the likelihood of things going wrong, and what to do when they do.

Every so often the manuals will need to be revised to take into account changes in the software used. Perhaps every year would be sufficient. Any additions to the software in the meantime could be covered by posters.

Posters and manuals should be replaced as soon as they start to look tatty. Apart from the inherent contradiction in a tatty poster asking people to keep the room tidy, keeping the appearance of all aspects of the room at a very high standard helps to get the message across about what your standards and expectations are. See Chapter 1 (the Hidden Curriculum section) and Chapter 5 (the section on Rules for the Computer Room) also.

Furniture required and its arrangement

Pupils need somewhere to store their work, and somewhere to work on things away from the computer.

Research has indicated that pupils learn more when they share a computer.

When setting up a computer room, or even when placing a single computer in a room, you should allow for the following furniture:

- benching or tables to put the computers on;
- stools or chairs;
- desks;
- a table for the printer, with plenty of space around it;
- somewhere to store uncollected print-outs temporarily;
- somewhere to store spare printer paper;
- somewhere to store unwanted print-outs before recycling – first, by using the other side of the paper for rough drawings etc, and secondly, by putting it into a recycle bag (but note that the recycle bag's obvious presence tends to lessen people's concern about wasting paper);
- somewhere to store worksheets;
- somewhere to store pupils' work;
- somewhere to store bags and coats;
- display boards.

How should the computers and desks be arranged? In an ideal situation:

- the computers should be arranged such that you can see everybody's monitor from wherever you are standing;
- desks for working away from the computers may be placed in clusters around the room, or centrally in the middle of the room.

Note that any arrangement will have health and safety implications (see below) and cost implications (eg of providing data and power points to the centre of the room).

Health and safety

Health and safety regulations change every so often, and so these notes should be taken as a general guide only. Always check the latest regulations before doing or buying anything. If you intend to set up a new computer room, or renovate an existing one, call in a company that has had dealings in the education sector. Always seek expert advice.

Electricity

- Extension leads should be avoided – install at least the required number of mains socket outlets.

- If desks are fitted with cable management systems, no more than six outlets should come from each desk, and the in-line desk unit fitted with a fuse rated at 7 amps maximum.

- Leads must not trail on the floor, or over the front or backs of desks or benching.

- Portable equipment should be inspected regularly, say a full safety test each year, and a visual check every few months. The mains lead must be treated as a separate item of equipment if it can be detached.

- Damaged equipment, such as cables and plugs, should be replaced by a qualified and authorised person only.

- As far as practicable, equipment should be turned off and unplugged from the wall socket when not in use.

Radiation emissions from VDUs

There continues to be debate about the effects of VDU radiation, for example during pregnancy. To be on the safe side, consider using low radiation monitors (which most new ones are anyway) and filter screens.

However, dust can be an irritant, so make sure that screens are cleaned on a regular basis, and that pupils and staff have regular and frequent breaks (see page 53).

Fire

Prevention is better than cure. Measures that can be taken include:

- using the proper fuses in plugs;
- using circuit breakers.

Fire extinguishers should be:

- based on carbon dioxide;
- positioned between the desks and the door, so that nobody has to move away from safety in order to pick up the fire extinguisher.

The working environment

Lighting

If the lighting is too bright it may cause fatigue. If too dim, it may cause people to screw their eyes up. Ideally, the light level should be at least 500 lux, according to British Standards.

Glare can also cause problems. To minimise glare:

- use non-glossy paint on walls;
- have non-reflective work surfaces;
- use window blinds;
- use screen filters (especially if the filters are non-reflective and are kept scrupulously clean);
- position the monitor at right angles to windows;
- adjust the contrast, brightness and background colour of the monitors; generally speaking, dark characters on a light background is better than the reverse as far as glare-reduction is concerned.

Heat

Computer equipment gives off heat. In a classroom with lots of computers and 20 or more pupils, the environment can become very unpleasant. To counteract this, make sure that the room is well-ventilated. This may require some form of air conditioning, in order to avoid drafts caused by open windows and doors.

If you are thinking of using a fan, take into account the fact that the noise from fans can be very distracting, especially if they are thermostatically controlled and so switch themselves on and off.

Switch equipment off when it is not in use, as far as it is practicable to do so.

Noise

Classrooms can be noisy at the best of times, and computer equipment can add to the hubbub. You can help to reduce it by taking the following steps:

- switch equipment off when it is not being used, in order to eradicate any background hum that it may give off;
- turn off the sounds made by some software;
- if software sounds are necessary, turn the volume down, or issue headphones (not earphones, which are a health hazard when shared), or locate the equipment away from other users.

Space

There should be enough space:

- for peripherals;
- for concept keyboards if necessary;
- for pupils to write on paper or in notebooks;
- for more than one pupil at a time;
- for the teacher to gain access to the computer;
- for pupils in wheelchairs;
- under the workstation for people's legs – an important consideration because insufficient leg room can lead to people accidentally pulling cables out with their feet;
- for the workstation to be situated away from radiators, which could prove very uncomfortable.

Equipment

- Equipment should be cleaned on a regular basis. See the section on maintenance routines in Chapter 5.
- Work surfaces should be large enough to hold documents comfortably.
- Work surfaces should be the correct height for the user. In the case of single computers, consider ordering height-adjustable computer trolleys.
- Chairs should be height- and tilt-adjustable.
- If the chairs have arms, the arms should allow pupils to sit close to the workstation, and with their arms horizontal.
- Chairs should allow users to sit with their thighs horizontal.
- If users have to adjust the height of the chairs such that their feet are off the ground, they should be provided with footrests.

- Monitors should be able to be tilted and swivelled to suit the user's preferences.
- Users should be able to adjust the screen's brightness and contrast.
- The screen resolution should be such that characters on the screen are both legible and of a high quality.
- Screen flicker should be avoided, by using monitors which have a refresh rate of at least 72 hertz (or 80 hertz to cater for users who are more sensitive to screen flicker than most).
- Monitors whose screens measure 15″ or more (diagonally) cause less eye strain than 14″.
- The keyboard should be separate from the computer and monitor, to enable it to be positioned to suit the user.
- The keyboard should be able to be tilted, which enables the user to adjust it in order to keep the hands and wrists in a horizontal position.
- There should be enough space in front of the keyboard to enable people to rest their hands.
- If you provide a wrist-rest to reduce the possibility of repetitive strain injury (RSI), you will probably have to provide guidance on how to use them, since incorrect use can lead to problems rather than reduce them.

Software

Perhaps surprisingly, health and safety regulations cover software design. This is explained by the fact that poorly designed software can cause people to work inefficiently, and thereby cause stress. This can have the knock-on effect of causing people to not take breaks as frequently as they should because they are concerned to complete their work.

Software should be:

- easy to use;
- suitable for the task;
- designed to minimise users' errors such as forgetting to save work when closing down;
- easy to trouble-shoot, especially through a built-in help system;

- accurate in its depiction of the printed result, ie, ideally –
  WYSIWYG – what you see is what you get.

Rest breaks

Short and frequent breaks are more effective than long and infrequent
ones. The following are more likely to apply to staff and pupils in
secondary schools and colleges, where lessons tend to be longer.

Users should:

- have a 5 to 10 minute break every 50 minutes;
- take the break away from the computer – this does not mean
  having pupils wandering around the classroom at random, but
  getting on with other work, such as planning the next stage or
  looking at paper-based resources such as magazines;
- take very short breaks of about 10 seconds. This means looking
  away from the screen regularly throughout the day;
- vary the kind of tasks they do, in order to vary their posture.

Posture

Users should aim for the following posture:

- lower arms horizontal;
- thighs horizontal;
- feet flat on floor or, if necessary, on a foot rest.

It is a good idea to put information about breaks and posture on the
walls near single computers in classrooms, and on the walls of
computer rooms.

Chapter 5
Maintenance and routines

Introduction

If you are a successful ICT manager, sooner or later the computer resources will be very widely used. The situation in an educational institution is, generally speaking, very different from that generally found in an office, as shown in the following table:

Table 5.1
Differences in computer use between offices and schools and colleges

Offices	Schools and colleges
One person per computer	Many students per computer
Small range of applications used by each person	Large range of applications used by each student
People have a sense of ownership of "their" computer	Students do not have a sense of ownership

In a situation like this, there is lots of potential for inconvenience:

- If computer rooms are used, demand is often greater than supply.

- Because of the absence of a sense of ownership, computer equipment can be damaged through negligence, or computer rooms left untidy.
- Staff and pupils may have to learn how to use a large number of programs.
- Printing started by one group of pupils may prevent another group of pupils from printing their work.

Part of your job as ICT manager is to ensure that people do feel a sense of ownership, and to minimise the potential for inconvenience arising from the other factors mentioned above. You can do so through effective management of the facilities, and by setting up routines.

Note that most of the suggestions below can be applied to stand-alone computers and clusters of computers as well as computer rooms.

Managing room use

Room booking forms

It should take only a few minutes to book a class into a computer room.

Booking forms are often designed by room. This is fine when there is only one computer room – in fact, it is really the only way of doing it. Unfortunately, when another computer room comes on stream, ICT managers quite naturally make the mistake of creating another room timetable just like the original one. However, all this does is effectively double the time it takes to find a free slot, and so is only justified if the computer rooms have very specialised uses (for example, one may be set up as a computer controlled music room).

A better way of designing a room booking form where there are two or more computer rooms, and where these are more or less interchangeable in terms of equipment and potential usage, is to organise it by time rather than by room.

If you think about it from the point of view of the staff who want to book a room, it is easier to look up the time in the week when you have the group concerned, or when you want to instruct the whole class at once, and then see if there is a room free, than to look up each room separately.

Here is an example of a room booking form where there is more than one computer room:

Computer Room Booking Form

Four Steps For Booking A Room

1 Look at the sheet with the **day** and **date** you want to book the room for.
2 Look up the **lessons** you want to book the room for.
3 Look across the grid to see which **room** (if any) is free.
4 Enter your details in the space provided: your name, your subject and the group. Note that this form consists of **three** pages per week.

Timetable for Computer Rooms for Week Beginning__/__/1999
Mondays

	Room C4	Room C5	Room C6
Lesson 1	F Bloggs IT 10A	J Soap IT 8C	
Lesson 2	J Soap IT 9C	F Bloggs IT 7B	H Grimes IT 7A
Lesson 3			
Lunch	Computer Club		
Lesson 4		J Soap IT 9D	H Grimes IT 7C
Lesson 5			
Twilight		Staff Drop-In Session	

Additional Information

Each room contains 15 fast Pentium comnputers, with a laser printer and a colour printer. Colour printing is available only by prior arrangement. In addition, there is a scanner in room C6, and a stand-alone multimedia computer on a trolley, based in room C5. (If you wish to book this for use in a non-computer room, please complete the Stand-alone Booking Form.)
The software includes Microsoft Office 2000 and a range of educational applications. For a full and up-to-date list of the software available, see the IT section of the staff room noticeboard.
Pupils will need a user identity and a password to be able to use the system. If anyone has forgotten their password, please ask them to log on as a guest user (see the instructions on each computer) and complete a Password Request Form.
The network is very reliable, but please have another lesson 'up your sleeve' just in case there is a power cut or something!
IT Technician: Extension 347 or ask the Office to page him/her.

Figure 5.1 – Computer room booking form (more than one room)

Stand-alone computers can also be bookable.

Where should you put the booking forms? The ideal arrangement is as follows:

- the booking forms for the whole year should be placed in a ring binder;
- this ring binder should be kept in a special section of the staff room;
- it should be divided into terms or half-terms, to make it easier for staff to find the section they require;
- there should be a large notice on the front of it reading 'Please do not remove this binder from the staff room'.

Note that many slots can be booked in advance in consultation with staff in order to ensure that the requirements of different classes or subjects are met.

Incidentally, when the dates for booking forms have passed, don't throw the forms away: they can be an invaluable means of research into how the computer rooms are being used. They can also be helpful in tracing which group was using a computer room at a particular time.

Rules for computer rooms

You need to have rules of conduct for the computer rooms that are additional to, or in some cases in place of, the usual classroom rules (subject to agreement by the senior management).

For example, there is usually one classroom rule to the effect that pupils must stay in their seats. However, you may want to create an atmosphere in which pupils can get out of their seats, without your permission, in order to get their work from a printer. In this case, it would be a good idea to have a rule which states that there must never be more than one person at the printer at a time.

In addition to the usual rules of behaviour, computer room rules must include references to the equipment, such as:

- close down the programs, and your computer, properly;
- if you are not sure how to do something, try looking in the manual or at the posters before asking your teacher;

- use print preview before printing your work;
- spell check your work before printing;
- print a draft copy first and check it thoroughly before printing your final copy;
- please tidy diskettes and paper before leaving the room;
- look after the equipment, which is there to be used by everybody;
- keep your password to yourself.

Express the rules in a positive rather than a negative way. There are three reasons for doing so:

- a list of negative rules may put teachers off taking classes into the computer rooms;
- people are more likely to remember things when they are expressed positively;
- negative rules tell pupils what not to do, but they do not tell them what behaviour is expected; positive rules state how to behave.

Put these rules on the walls, and on the computers themselves, on a card.

INSET

Do not assume that staff who look after their own classrooms will also look after yours. Sometimes the worry experienced at the thought of being in a computer room is apparently enough to make teachers forget basic rules of classroom management.

Usually, this can all be changed with just a one-off INSET session lasting no longer than one hour. In fact, it is a good idea to have it agreed as part of the school's ICT policy that before staff bring a class into a computer room, they are expected to have undergone your training, or to have been trained by someone who has.

This may sound rather tyrannical, but it is no different in principle to the practice that health clubs have of requiring people to have an introductory training session in the gym before being allowed to use it unaccompanied. The computer room, after all, contains potentially dangerous equipment – and certainly very expensive equipment – and it is not unreasonable to ask staff to undergo an hour's training in order to be able to take a lesson in it.

It is a good idea to reinforce this by providing the teacher who does the cover with a list of people who have undergone the training, along with a request to use them (and the IT department) as far as possible for cover lessons in computer rooms. (This advice only applies to primary schools insofar as long-term absence is concerned, when they can try to use substitute teachers who have a good understanding of ICT.)

It would also be a good idea to establish the training as part of the induction process for new staff and trainee teachers.

Ideally, the training should cover the following:

- starting up and closing down;
- print management;
- basic trouble-shooting;
- pupil movement;
- looking after the equipment;
- health and safety issues;
- routines for entering and leaving the room.

Monitoring room and software use

It is a good idea to monitor room and software use for the following reasons:

- you can see which staff or departments are making the most use of the computer rooms, which could be quite important if you have to evaluate bids for computer equipment;
- you may need to track down who was using the room at a particular time;
- you may be able to spot a pattern of room usage which could help in future planning;
- you will be able to chart the growth (hopefully) of computer room usage over time;
- if you can monitor software use as well, this can help you to plan future purchases.

It is a worthwhile investment to buy software, perhaps as part of the network, that will automatically monitor room usage, software use, printing and programs used by individual users.

This last one can be very powerful. In one school, a parent complained that her son had been given an unduly low level in IT because he was always using the computer room after school and at lunchtime. A quick look at the database revealed that this was true – but that on virtually every occasion he had been using Paintbrush or Solitaire.

Software that monitors printing is in itself an excellent investment, especially if it can easily be configured to give pupils credits. The way the system works is that you give pupils a certain number of credits per week. You then give each page a cost, in terms of credits. This enables you to set different 'prices' on different types of printers.

The software can usually be set up to prevent a print job going ahead at all if the user does not have enough credits. This helps to prevent the situation where someone 'accidentally' prints 35 copies of a 10 page document.

Despite the usefulness of monitoring programs – or auditing or management programs as they're often known – it is still worthwhile keeping the old booking forms for a while (say an academic year). That is because they enable you to see the picture in a way that a computer print-out is often unable to.

Labelling the computers

It is essential to number each computer, for the following reasons:

- it makes it easy for people to identify a computer that is 'playing up'; it is much easier to say 'number 13' than to say 'the third one on the left from the second window';
- it makes it easy to give visitors logging on instructions; for example, you can tell them that if they use computer number 3, they should log on as guest3;
- it makes it easier for you to keep track of stock;
- it helps you to keep track of equipment you loan out or put into classrooms.

It is a good idea to label each computer with rules or instructions as well as the number. Here is an example of such a label, which need be only A6 in size (ie half of A5):

Workstation number 24

If you do not know your user identity, please log on to this workstation as: **GUEST24** *and the password* **GUEST24.**

If you need help, try using:

- *The posters on the walls.*
- *The manual next to this workstation.*
- *The Help in the program you are using.*

IMPORTANT ...

When you are finished, please:

- *Log off properly – don't just switch the computer off.*
- *Clear any rubbish away from the table and floor.*
- *Put your chair/stool back properly.*
- *Check that you have all your belongings.*

Figure 5.2 – Example of a computer label

Running a computer club

This is an activity which clearly has implications for the use of the computer facilities. You must ask yourself a series of questions before starting, rather than just open the computer room doors at lunchtime or after school or college.

- What is the aim of the club? For example, relaxation through playing computer games; learning extra skills not covered in the scheme of work; extra practice at skills covered in lessons; homework.
- On what basis will pupils be admitted? For example, first come, first served; certain days of the week according to their year group; progress or lack of it.
- Who will run the club? Will pupils take part in the running of the club?

Normal computer room rules should apply, and not be relaxed because the activities are outside normal lessons. For instance, you should refrain from eating your lunch in the computer room in order to open the room 15 minutes earlier.

On-demand access

It is becoming increasingly accepted and expected for pupils to be able to access computers before and after school, during the lunch break, and during free lessons. You still need to address certain issues, such as:

- Are the health and safety rules being observed? Pupils need to be supervised. In a secondary school, it may be possible for staff to be asked to cover learning areas in non-contact time.
- How is the equipment being supervised?

Booking mobile equipment

You may be in a position to 'hire out' equipment to staff, such as a computer system on a trolley. This can be a good way of giving classes access to a computer which they might not otherwise have enjoyed.

The booking form for the mobile system should also be kept in a central location.

You will need to ensure that the computer system and peripherals, and CD-ROMs etc are checked before and after use.

Loaning equipment to staff

Much of the advice in this section is based on loaning computers, but the general principles apply to all items.

Staff often wish to borrow equipment, especially laptops. You may find it easier to loan equipment over weekends and holiday periods rather than during the week. For reasons that will become clear, it is a good idea to invest not only in virus-checking software, but also software that keeps track of what programs have been installed and uninstalled – or that locks down the computer to prevent anyone installing or uninstalling software.

Staff who borrow equipment should be made aware of the following, perhaps by asking them to sign a declaration that they agree to the conditions:

- programs should not be installed or uninstalled, partly because of possible copyright implications, and partly because of potential damage to system files;

- the equipment may not be covered by insurance off the premises, in which case it will have to be replaced by the member of staff if it is lost or stolen;

- the equipment must be returned by the time and date, and to the room, specified.

When you loan equipment, do the following:

- test it to ensure that it is working properly;

- run a virus check;

- complete a sheet or book with details of the name of the member of staff, item borrowed, serial number, date borrowed, date to be returned, and an indication that the item was checked and found to be ok;

- ensure that the teacher understands the conditions on which the item is being lent, such as the insurance considerations as mentioned above.

When people return equipment, do the following:

- test it to ensure that it is working properly;

- run a virus check;

- check that no additional software has been installed;

- indicate on the booking sheet that the item has been returned and that it is working properly.

Community access

If you wish to make your computer facilities available to the community at large, there are a number of things to consider:

- Will the access be on a drop-in basis, or at set times?

- Will the facilities be used on a formal basis, such as through a course, or an informal basis?

- Taking into account the answers to the previous questions, what supervision arrangements will be in place?

- If community access is to be informal, how will people be trained to use the system?

- Will users have their own personal user identities, individual but general user identities (such as Guest1, Guest2 etc) or a group user identity?

- How will you address security issues associated with having adults on site?

- On what basis will members of the community be permitted to use the facilities?

- Is there scope for the school or college earning extra money by hiring the facilities to local companies for training purposes?

- How will parents and other members of the community be informed of developments in ICT? By newsletter? By open evenings?

Note that it does not always pay to advertise. If you keep the community informed of developments in ICT, especially hardware and software purchases, it is even more important to ensure that physical security issues are addressed (see Chapter 3).

Maintenance routines

Managing computer rooms entails constant maintenance. To some extent you can make the rooms 'self-maintaining' by establishing good practice along the lines suggested below. However, you will need to develop routines for keeping the rooms in good order.

The complete list of tasks that have to be done to keep the computer rooms looking and working well is somewhat overwhelming. You can make it more manageable by breaking it down into tasks which must be done:

- every day;
- every week;
- each month;
- each holiday;
- each year;
- on a random basis; and
- in response to fault reports.

If you do not have a technician, the following list of tasks provides good reasons why you need one. Note that network management and managed services are covered in Chapter 9.

Tasks which must be done every day

The daily routines listed below help to ensure that the computer rooms are respected by other users, as well as ensuring that they are fully functional.

It is annoying to have to clear up a room after another member of staff has used it. However, it is self-defeating to refuse to clear up after people, because if the room looks untidy when the next class comes in, the pupils there will not have high standards to maintain either. Staff using computers should check that:

- there is ample printer paper in each printer at the start of each morning and afternoon session;
- there is no rubbish on the floor, especially near the printers;
- workstations are tidy, eg no mice dangling down from work bench;
- posters are not hanging off the walls;
- help sheets and manuals are in place, and that damaged ones are replaced;
- the server is backed up.

Tasks which must be done every week

It is frustrating to discover that a particular computer or printer has not worked for the past three weeks. Staff should be encouraged to report faults (see page 68) as they occur. These routines should help you to achieve that goal.

Although they sound daunting, remember that tasks can be done on different days: room 1 can be checked on Mondays, the library checked on Tuesday and so on. In this way, the weekly routine is incorporated into the daily routine. Check that:

- all mice have mouse balls;
- the printers work;

- all computers boot up properly;
- the internet connection works;
- there are adequate stocks of printer paper;
- there is a record of stock used, which will assist you in requesting money for spending on ICT next year;
- unused or guest files are deleted.

Tasks which must be done each month

You should clean all of the following *at least* monthly, and preferably weekly:

- *monitors*: for health and safety reasons;.
- *keyboards*: as well as being a health matter, dirty keyboards are off-putting, and do not encourage people to look after the equipment;
- *mice*: because if you don't, they won't work very well.

You will find it easier to cope if you have a rota in which a different room has its equipment cleaned each week.

Tasks which must be done each holiday

There are tasks which are best done when you are unlikely to be disturbed. If you do not have a technician, you may like to prevent all computer room bookings on the last day or two of each term. If you give ample notice of the days when each computer room will be out of action, there should not be too much of a problem. You should do this when you create the computer room booking forms at the beginning of the year.

Technicians usually work on a different contract, one that requires them to be around for part of the holidays. If so, you can make sure the routines below are undertaken in the holidays, thereby cutting down on computer 'down time' during the term.

You should:

- check computers for 'rogue' programs;
- check that computer systems are where they are supposed to be, if you placed computer equipment in classrooms;

- clean the computers (monitors, keyboards and mice) that are around the building.

Tasks which must be done each year

Each year you should:

- call in loaned equipment for checking and cleaning;
- check all licences, ie that you have the right number of licences for each item of software, and that there are no unlicensed programs in use;
- do a complete stock check;
- order sufficient quantities of printer paper, toner etc.

Tasks which must be done on a random basis

The term 'random' is used here to refer to tasks that you cannot set a definite time aside for on a regular basis, not just tasks which you cannot plan for. (In fact, you should plan for unplanned events such as the server crashing, by trying to make sure there is enough time to sort the problem out. If you do not have a technician, or external maintenance support, and have a full timetable, other staff may have to resign themselves to problems taking longer to deal with than might be considered ideal.)

Random tasks include:

- replacing toner cartridges as required (keep a record of paper and toner used, because that will help you plan your purchasing over the year and will also alert you if too much seems to be being used in a particular area);
- checking for unlicensed software, especially on laptops or other loaned computers.

Stock recording and checking

Recording and checking includes the following:

- a routine for logging new equipment when it arrives, and before it is put into use – logging new equipment means recording when it arrived, its serial number, and perhaps giving it a number of your own for fast identification; it also means noting where it has been put;

- finding out what the standard school, college or LEA approved stock recording method is, and using it; this should not preclude you from using your own system, especially if it is better in some way; for example, you may be able to buy or develop a bar-coding program that will make stock checking very fast;
- undertaking spot checks every so often, even if you are required to undertake a stock check just once a year, as computer equipment has a habit of being moved about from one room to another;
- responding to unplanned events such as a break-in or the server crashing.

Many stock recording systems in use are paper-based, and these have their limitations. If you were to record your equipment in a database or a spreadsheet, you would very easily be able to generate lists of particular items, or the equipment in a particular room.

Responding to fault reports

The first thing you have to understand about faults is that everyone regards their own one as urgent. You must have a system of reporting faults and of dealing with them. If you do not devise a system, people will just stop you in the corridor, and you could easily end up chasing your own tail.

The way of dealing with faults should include encouraging people to do their own trouble-shooting. It is probably true to say that most 'faults' arise through not having plugged something in, or something of that nature. For a technician to discover and rectify this could easily take between 15 minutes and half an hour. You don't have to be a mathematician to realise that a technician could easily spend all day dealing with a dozen or so very trivial 'faults' while other, more serious, problems remain unresolved.

Ways of dealing with computer-related faults include the following:

- devise a trouble-shooting guide to cover the most common faults; see Figure 5.3 for an example of a trouble-shooting guide;

Trouble-shooting guide

Computer doesn't work

Is it plugged in?

Is it connecgted to the monitor?

Is it switched on?

Is the monitor switched on?

Monitor doesn't work

Is it plugged in?

Is it connected to the computer?

Is it switched on?

Are brightness and contrast controls properly adjusted?

Printer does't work

Is it connected to the computer or file server?

Is it switched on?

Is there paper in it?

Is the 'on line' light on?

Are the print options set correctly – eg, are you trying to print to the correct printer?

Figure 5.3 – *Example of a trouble-shooting guide*

- devise a fault reporting form, and make sure that there are plenty of these in the rooms where they are needed, and in the staff room; see figure 5.4 for an example of a fault report form;

- enter the fault in a record book, along with details such as the date it was reported, and who by, and the date you investigated the problem, and the outcome; not only will this help you if you have to call an engineer, but if you leave it in the staffroom people can check on the progress of the faults they reported; see figure 5.5 for an example of a fault record form.

Computer Fault Report Form

Name:_____

Computer Number: _____

Program in use: _____

Please note EXACTLY any error messages that appeared on the screen:

_____

_____

_____

_____

Please describe what happened:

_____

_____

What are you doing, or trying to do, at the time?

_____

_____

_____

Please leave this section blank

Seen by: _____ Date:_____

Likely cause: _____

Action taken:_____

Figure 5.4 – *Example of a fault-reporting form*

Computer Number	Date Reported	Date seen	Problem	Cause	Fixed?	Action Taken

Figure 5.5 – Example of a fault record form

Helping others to help you

You can make life easier for yourself by making it easy for staff to maintain computers you have lent them, and difficult for staff or pupils to damage the equipment or cause it to break down.

For example, when you lend someone a computer you can:

- give them a checklist of dos and don'ts regarding the use of the computer;
- give them a set of screen wipes for cleaning the monitor, and a set of instructions about why and how they should use them on a regular basis;
- 'lock down' the computer so that it is very difficult for anyone to install software without your authorisation.

Lesson routines in rooms containing computers

The recommended routines for lessons in rooms containing computers are essentially just the same as those for any lesson.

Entering and leaving computer rooms

Pupils should:

- line up quietly outside the room, and go in only when the teacher tells them to;
- not get food and drink out;
- **walk** into and out of the room rather than run into it;
- make sure they have shut down the computers properly at the end of the session;
- make sure that their workstations are left tidy.

Start and end of lessons

If you have a network, and all the pupils log on at the same time, or start the same program at once, the network – especially if it is an older system – may slow down. You need to have an activity that the class can do before the system has finished booting up or loading the program.

Computers can break down for all kinds of reasons. Although computers and computer networks are becoming more and more robust, it is wise to assume that the worst is going to happen. In other words, be prepared with a non-computer based activity that will last for the whole lesson if necessary. Encourage others to do so too – perhaps by leading by example.

Be prepared for pupils forgetting their passwords, or for unexpected new arrivals who have not yet been given a user identity. See 'User management' below.

Printing

Printing can be both disruptive and wasteful, and so you need to establish rules to govern it.

Ideally, you should have at least one printer in each room containing a computer. If you have stand-alone computers around the building, each should either have its own printer or be connected to a nearby printer.

It is a good idea to invest in printer management software which enables you to:

- set printing limits in the form of 'credits' for each user or group of users;
- assign a cost to each credit to allow you to charge individuals and groups;
- keep a record of who is printing what, and where, in order to make it easier to plan where to locate extra printers.

Before buying printer management software, ask for details of reference sites that use the same computer systems as you do. The software can be quite costly, and so you need to be sure that it will work properly before buying it.

If you have installed what is called a 'value-added' network, ie one that has management tools on top of the basic operating system, you will probably already have printer management software included.

Printer management software, by helping to reduce paper wastage, can pay for itself in a relatively short time in schools and colleges where a great deal of printing is done.

Establish certain rules of good conduct, and encourage other staff to do the same. Users should:

- put their name on each sheet, eg as a header;
- do a spell check if the software allows;
- use the print preview feature;
- print drafts in draft mode and/or the least expensive printer (eg a laser printer rather than a colour inkjet);
- not collect around the printer waiting for their work – if the whole class is printing graphics over the network, some people could waste the whole lesson waiting;
- not start printing within the last ten minutes of the lesson.

User management

User identities

It is important to set up procedures which make it easy to keep everything running smoothly. This section suggests some ideas.

Change the default administrator's password immediately, and make sure someone else, whom you can trust, knows it. It is a good idea to create another user with administrative privileges in case the default one cannot gain access to the system at any time.

The network manager should have at least two user identities: administrator, and ordinary user. The former should be used only for administration-related tasks. Having a separate user identity for ordinary work cuts out the risk of accidentally deleting system files.

It is important to set up a system of creating user identities which are:

- logical, so that staff and pupils can work them out;

- easy to create, automatically if necessary;
- unique;
- easy to delete in a batch, such as when pupils in a particular year leave.

There are several approaches to this, as summarised below. Suppose there are two pupils with the same name – Fred Bloggs, in Year 5, and Fred Bloggs, in Year 6. Here are a few different approaches:

Table 5.2
Alternative approaches to network user identities

Microsoft solution:	*FredB*	*FredB1*
Variant on Microsoft solution:	*FredB1*	*FredB2*
Alternative approach 1:	*FredB*	*FredB*
Alternative approach 2:	*94FredB*	*95FredB*

The Microsoft solution and its variant can both be generated, at least to some extent, within a reasonably high-powered spreadsheet. These options satisfy the requirements that user identities are derived logically, that they are easy to create and that they are unique.

However, they do not automatically satisfy the requirement of being able to delete a whole year group at a time. To achieve this, you would need to keep a list of pupils' names and their user identities in a file whose name clearly indicated which year they were in.

Alternative approach 1 is a non-starter as a policy. Even if the network management software allows you to create duplicate names, which is highly unlikely, this can lead to all sorts of problems, including files being saved in the wrong directory.

If, however, you are creating your user identities manually, it is easy to create duplicate names accidentally. You can check for duplicate names either manually or by pasting the names into a spreadsheet set up for the purpose, since it is possible to insert formulae that will check for duplicate entries.

Alternative approach 2 makes it easy to identify the year in which a pupil entered the school, but does not conform to Microsoft's criteria. It is possible to combine this approach with the Microsoft one or its variant.

Passwords

If you use a network, check the default password settings. In some, it is the word 'password', whilst in others it is the same as the user identity. It may be possible for you to specify users' passwords, or you may be able to allow them to change their own passwords.

If you allow users to change their passwords, you have to be prepared for them to forget their new password. If you do not allow them to change their password, and the default password is used, you lose the benefit of having passwords. A compromise solution is to allow pupils to change their passwords once, and then reset their network privileges to prevent them changing them again.

It is important to keep a list of pupils and their user identities and passwords, and to ensure that teaching staff have copies, or access to the information.

Pupils without user identities

Sometimes pupils arrive without there having been time to put them on the system. Ideally, you should set up spare user identities for such an eventuality. These can also be used by pupils who have forgotten their passwords, although this raises the issue of transferring their work into their own area at a later date (unless the work they do need not be saved, or they are asked to do non-computer work).

When you do put new pupils on the system, ensure that they are allocated to the year group (if appropriate) that they would have been in had they entered the school at the same time as their peers.

User management for stand-alones

It is often possible to have user identity systems and passwords for stand-alone systems as well as networks. For example, in turnkey systems such as the RM Window Box, the system is supplied with three user identities: administrator, teacher and pupil. These differ from each other in terms of access to system files and various facilities. You may be able to set up extra user identities, but user management can soon become unmanageable if you have several stand-alone systems.

Diskette and CD-ROM management

If you use stand-alone systems, you will need to consider how to manage CD-ROMs and diskettes. Ideally, pupils should be made responsible for their own diskettes, but this is not always feasible, and sometimes pupils will forget to bring their diskette along.

CD-ROMs should be itemised in your stock book. If you have multiple copies of some titles, number the CD-ROMs.

You need to establish a system that will enable you to trace who last had a missing or damaged CD-ROM.

For some work, and in some circumstances, it is possible to have a class diskette. If you keep a set of diskettes for pupils and/or classes, make sure that they are numbered, and that you have a file containing details of diskette allocations.

Diskettes will need to be:

- virus checked;
- backed up;
- cleared every so often;
- checked at the start and end of lessons.

Chapter 6
Managing achievement in IT

General considerations

Process and accountability

Raising achievement in any subject does not come about as a result of just one or two factors in isolation. Rather, there needs to be an approach which centres on both process and accountability.

By 'process' we mean the setting up of procedures to help ensure that pupil achievement is likely to be raised. The term 'accountability' refers to the fact that, as Roger Luxton, Principal Inspector of Barking and Dagenham LEA has put it, good processes are of little use if they do not lead to good outcomes.

> **(INSET lecture, 'Managing Pupil Achievement', 20 September 1996).**

Consequently, subject co-ordinators and Heads of Department are responsible for knowing what teaching and learning is going on, and what progress (if any) is being made. These days, the bottom line consideration can be thought of in terms of: are pupils getting good value for money in return for their parents' taxes?

Factors which contribute to the raising of achievement

The ICT manager should:

- have a clear idea of the place of IT and ICT in the curriculum, and be able to communicate this to others;

- have a clear approach to the raising of achievement, such as the adoption of a suitable scheme of work (see 'IT lessons' below); but...

- ...be prepared to be flexible enough to allow others to contribute their ideas, because even non-experts and trainee teachers often come up with interesting ideas on how to approach a particular topic, or how to address the problem of 'failing' pupils;

- have high expectations of both pupils and staff;

- be an expert in the subject, in the sense of having a clear understanding of what IT is all about, and a good general knowledge of the research that has been undertaken, current topics of debate, likely future developments and so on.

IT lessons

Constructing schemes of work

When you construct a scheme of work you need to keep in mind three main ideas:

- what skills and understanding the pupils have acquired already;
- what the pupils will know by the end of their current year;
- what they will know by the end of the Key Stage.

The first one is very important. If you do not get this right, members of the class will be out of their depth, or under-stretched. You can address the problem by adopting one or more of the following approaches, depending on your particular circumstances:

- If you are in a secondary school, liaise with IT Co-ordinators from feeder schools, either directly or through the LEA, time and other resources permitting.

- As a variation on the above, work with all of the IT Co-ordinators in your area to produce a joint scheme of work that spans all four Key Stages – one such approach is described by Paul Fenton ('Vertical Integration', *InTegrate*, January 1996); it relies for its success on every institution in the area releasing its ICT manager for a day when necessary.

- Adopt, or adapt, the LEA scheme of work, if there is one; if all schools did so, then every school or college would, in theory, have a good idea of what the pupils coming to them have covered.

Ultimately, however, it is unwise to rely on schemes of work as evidence of skills acquired. Unless lessons have been observed and appropriate action taken where necessary, there is no guarantee that what is laid down in the scheme of work is what is actually being covered in the classroom.

A well-planned scheme of work starts with the big picture and becomes more and more detailed. See, for example, the *Informatics* Course sold by the National Association of Co-ordinators and Teachers of IT (ACITT). In fact, there are several stages involved, which can be summarised by the following questions:

1 What should the pupils know at the end of this Key Stage (or at the end of their course)?

2 What should the pupils know by the end of this academic year?

3 What should the pupils know by the end of each term (or the end of each Unit)?

4 What should the pupils know by the end of each lesson?

5 What scenarios can be used as a vehicle for teaching these skills?

6 What links to other areas of the curriculum can be forged?

7 Are pupils given increasing opportunities to choose the software to solve a problem?

8 Are pupils given increasing opportunities to integrate several kinds of program? (An effective way of achieving this is to set projects which become more and more open-ended as the course progresses. Some element of choice can be built in to the scheme of work at the primary school level also.)

9 Where IT is delivered in a wholly cross-curricular way, is the IT to be taught independent of the subject matter? (For example, presentation skills using word processing software can be taught whatever the subject or topic. The scheme of work in these circumstances can still be set out in Units, but these Units will not be time-based. Also, the lessons which comprise the Units will either be content-free or contain suggestions for activities and subject matter. The QCA Scheme of Work is an example of this approach: QCA/DfEE, *Information Technology: A scheme of work for Key Stages 1 and 2*, 1998. See also Barking & Dagenham, *Problem solving with IT: Year group targets for Key Stages 1 and 2*, 1995.)

10 What resources are required for the delivery of each Unit?

11 What staff training is required?

12 What evidence of pupil attainment will be required?

13 What homework will be set throughout the Unit?

14 How does each Unit link with previous and following Units to ensure progression and consistency?

15 How does each Unit address the IT Programme of Study?

It is tempting to suggest a scheme of work in these pages, but it would be my scheme of work, not yours. By working out the answers to

IT Scheme of Work for Year:

Term	PoS Addressed	Activity	Resources needed	Extension work	Pre-requisite	Subject links
1.1						
1.2						
2.1						
2.2						
3.1						
3.2						

Figure 6.1 – Example of a scheme of work pro forma

these questions, you are far more likely to come up with the right scheme of work for your particular circumstances.

One way of managing the process of devising a scheme of work is to devise the Units or activities for one year at a time, using a pro forma such as the one shown in Figure 6.1.

Lesson planning

Lesson planning for IT is not that different from any other subject. Lessons should:

- have clear learning objectives;
- have minimum targets set. This means saying that by the end of this lesson, all pupils in this class will have learnt 'X'. For example, in database work, the minimum target might be that all pupils learn the vocabulary, such as 'field'. See the QCA scheme mentioned above for a variation of this approach. Minimum target setting is a good way of ensuring that all pupils achieve a certain level of understanding, and provides benchmarks. There is a danger, however, that targets can be set too low;
- be part of a wider scheme of work;
- make good use of the resources available;
- have built-in revision and extension activities, ie this should take differentiation into account;
- be accessible to all pupils in the class: this will entail thinking carefully about the resources used;
- take into consideration the possibility of technical problems.

If you run a Unit-based scheme of work, and there are several staff involved in its delivery, consider asking individual staff to take responsibility for a Unit. This approach can be quite good because:

- staff are 'forced' to think about the pedagogical aspects of teaching the subject rather than getting bogged down in the technicalities;
- staff quite often come up with good ideas that one person (you) may not have thought of;
- it gives staff some ownership of the Units in the scheme of work;

- it provides opportunities for staff development;
- it can reduce your workload.

You may find it easier to manage lesson preparation and ensure consistency of approach if you devise a lesson plan template for use by all the staff concerned.

Homework management

Homework can and should be set for pupils, even for younger ones. Setting homework is important because:

- it helps pupils prepare for the lesson, and thereby get the most benefit from using the computers in class;
- it can reinforce and extend the work done in lessons;
- it gets across the idea that IT is not just about computers: it involves thinking too;
- if other subjects have homework, IT homework must be set too if the subject is to be taken seriously.

To ensure that pupils obtain the greatest benefit from homework, it should be:

- planned as part of the lesson and/or Unit preparation;
- known and published in advance;
- set consistently to all classes;
- marked promptly;
- marked with comments.

Managing homework therefore consists of three main activities:

- planning;
- setting;
- marking.

Homework should be planned as part of the lesson or Unit. If the subject is being delivered in a wholly cross-curricular way, homework should still be set as part of the scheme of work being followed. In those circumstances, you will need to suggest a range of activities that would be applicable whatever the context of the lesson.

Homework should be set early in the lesson, not in the last 2 minutes when everyone is concentrating on packing up. Give the homework out near the start of the lesson, taking time to make sure that everyone has written it down correctly, understands what they have to do, and knows when it has to be handed in. Consider giving out a sheet consisting of every homework at the start of the course. If there is a school or college intranet, homework assignments can be posted there.

Commenting on homework is time-consuming. If circumstances allow, you can look at homework with individual pupils during the lesson while the rest of the group is doing the work set. Working in this way enables you to gain more insight into the pupil's thinking processes, and helps to establish rapport between you and the members of the class.

Management of non-computer work

Not all IT can be taught through using a computer. Often, before someone can understand what they are doing on a computer, they have to be able to relate it to their own experience, or to work through the problem without a computer first in order to understand the processes involved.

You need to take account of this when planning room layout (because there should be space to work away from the computer), lesson preparation and purchasing requirements. Examples of resources include:

- record cards for database work;
- database planning sheets;
- spreadsheet planning sheets;
- text books and worksheets;
- exercise books or paper;
- plain paper and crayons/felt tip pens.

Managing the use of computer games

Even games which are not intended to be educational can be. For example, Solitaire is very useful for helping people to master the main aspects of using a mouse, such as dragging and double-clicking.

However, using games like this should either be planned for as part of lessons, or made available only at certain times of the day (you can do this quite easily on most networks).

Other games include word searches and other non-computer games. These can be used as revision aids, reward activities, or as a more central part of the lesson. Their use must be planned for, and stocks maintained. You will need to file the resources by age group and subject.

IT in the curriculum

Reinforcing IT in other subjects

If you teach IT as a discrete subject, other subjects provide an opportunity for pupils to apply what they have learnt.

You can help to manage this by:

- informing staff what you have just covered, and are about to cover, in the IT course, which is easy to do if you are running a Unit-based course;
- making sure that other staff know the policies on various aspects of ICT, such as use of correct terminology, or printing. (The terminology to be used should be included in the scheme of work.)

Enhancing other subjects through IT (ICT)

The Programmes of Study for the other National Curriculum subjects specify the use of IT. At the time of writing, there are proposals to replace the requirements for other subjects to use IT 'as appropriate' with more specific ones.

You can help to manage the use of IT in other subjects by:

- running INSET on the use of IT in various subjects;
- informing staff of relevant courses run by the LEA or other bodies;
- encouraging staff to build ICT into their schemes of work and

IT Order (KS2|)	Unit or Activity	Taught by	When
1a			
1b			
1c			
1d			
2a			
2b			
2c			
2d			

Figure 6.2 – *Example of an IT plan*

lesson plans as an integral part of the course, not as an added extra;

■ informing staff of what resources, including web sites, are available in their subject.

Teaching IT through other subjects

With this approach you need to agree a plan of who will do what, and when. Figure 6.2 shows an example of such a plan. See also Figure 7.2 (page 93).

It is essential to ensure that:

- if staff need to use a computer room to deliver their part of the IT curriculum, the room is booked well in advance;
- staff know and understand the expected IT learning outcomes of the course as a whole, and individual Units and lessons;
- staff are given relevant INSET at an early stage: they may need INSET on the software, the scheme of work, IT concepts and assessing IT;
- staff deliver what they have agreed to deliver – a pupil's coverage of the curriculum should not depend on who teaches him or her; this will entail meetings with other staff, moderation of coursework and, if possible, lesson observation;
- if, at Key Stage 3 or above, departments teach IT through their own schemes of work, rather than using their time to teach the IT scheme of work, that the work they intend to do is sufficiently challenging and IT-oriented;
- pupils have access to computers outside formal lessons – and, of course, in lessons:

It is imperative to ensure that resources are easy to book and that assistance is either on hand or easily called. If staff have a bad experience early on in their ICT ventures, they will not wish to pursue the matter, or will do so with an obvious lack of enthusiasm.

The role of an ICT Committee

Many schools and colleges have found it useful to establish an ICT Committee. Although committees can be notorious for holding up the decision-making process, or for coming up with compromises that satisfy nobody, they can be useful. This is especially true when the ICT manager is a one-person band, as is often the case in schools.

The ICT Committee can help you manage ICT by:

- providing a talking shop for ideas about the delivery of IT, distribution of hardware and so on;
- assisting with the construction of the IT scheme of work;
- helping to identify subject areas where parts of the IT scheme of work could be delivered or exemplified;

- assisting in undertaking audits of staff IT skills, and similar exercises;
- helping to run staff INSET;
- helping to run computer clubs and similar activities;
- planning and administering community access;
- spreading good practice in other subject areas;
- lobbying members of the senior management team;
- making representations to the Governing Body.

Managing certification

Pupils often find it an incentive to work towards certification. This may be in the form of an internal or external qualification. The 'qualification' can be as simple as a certificate stating that a certain level of proficiency has been achieved.

Managing the certification process involves making sure that:

- pupils know and understand the criteria for gaining the certificate;
- there is an 'upgrade' path, either to a more comprehensive certificate, or to an external qualification;
- at Key Stage 3 and above, there is a clear link between your course and external qualifications;
- that any accreditation has to be earned, not given out like confetti (although you will have to have different criteria for different pupils).

As far as external accreditation is concerned, there is a wide range of options on offer, ranging from basic skills tests to GCSE and above. Contact the main Examination Boards for further details.

OFSTED

Pre-OFSTED preparation

There are a number of things you can do to make the process of being inspected as painless as possible. It is a good idea to:

- make sure your ICT Policy and other documentation (see Chapter 2) is both up-to-date and accessible;

- have a grid/timetable available showing what IT is being taught or used where and at what time;
- make sure that marking is kept up to date;
- ensure that lesson plans, including homework, are available;
- if possible, ask your LEA advisory service to do a pre-inspection visit – although you will probably have to pay for it.

Note that part of the evidence that inspectors look for is the way pupils treat the computer facilities, which is why the hidden curriculum (Chapter 1) and regular maintenance (Chapter 5) are so important.

During the inspection

It is very easy to become defensive when being quizzed by inspectors. The best strategy, although perhaps easier said than done, is to keep cool and be honest. Nobody expects you to be perfect, and it is probably true to say that if you are seen to be addressing problems in the IT provision that will be a definite point in your favour.

Post-OFSTED planning

At the end of the inspection process, you will probably receive oral feedback, and within 6 weeks the final report will be published. Hopefully, any problems noted will be ones that you have recognised and started to address already.

Look at the problems that need to be addressed, and draw up an action plan. Figure 6.3 below is an example of an action plan pro forma.

Problem	Action needed	By when	By when	Success Criteria

Figure 6.3 – Example of an action plan pro forma

Chapter 7
Managing the recording and assessment of IT

Managing record-keeping

As a teacher you will need to keep records of:

- pupils' marks;
- work handed in and work outstanding;
- work covered in lessons;
- homework set.

Where IT is delivered as a discrete subject, record-keeping is easier than when it is delivered across the curriculum. In fact, there is no difference between discrete IT and any other subject, except that you may want to keep examples of pupils' computer-based work done outside IT lessons, such as in other subjects or at home.

Methods of keeping records

You may prefer to keep records in a mark book, or in ring binders. The **advantages** of using ring binders are:

- you can have one for each year group or course you teach;
- you are not limited to pre-formatted grids, and so can insert more information;
- it is easy to put in extra information and take out extraneous sheets.

The **disadvantages** of using ring binders are:

- they can be awkward to carry;
- they tend to break open at the most inconvenient times!

If you use a mark book only, you will probably need to insert cross-references to your scheme of work. This makes it easier to write meaningful details in the small space provided. For example, you can write 'U2L3H' for Unit 2 Lesson 3 Homework.

Date	Work planned	Work completed	Homework set	Comments
17 March 1999	Unit 3 Lesson 4	Up to section 2 point 5	Homework #7	Revise terminology at start of next lesson

Figure 7.1 – Lesson record sheet

Figure 7.1 shows an example of a lesson record sheet.

An additional, or alternative, approach to record keeping is to use a spreadsheet to record students' marks. Although this can be inconvenient, and often slower than keeping a paper-based system, the spreadsheet approach has the following distinct **advantages**:

- It is easy to calculate average marks both for individuals and whole classes.
- Where relevant, you can set the spreadsheet up to work out predicted grades.

■ You can use the spreadsheet as a basis for a reporting system based on mail-merging techniques.

Recording work covered across the curriculum is not quite as easy, but can be done. You will probably find it useful to maintain two types of document:

■ a record of work done in different classes or subjects;
■ a record of work done by each pupil or student.

Recording work done in other subjects

Figure 7.2 shows an example of a record sheet for work done in each class or subject. (This can, in fact, be the same as the curriculum plan, with ticks to show what has been covered.) You may prefer to amend this sheet such that the Units or activities are described, or refer to subject schemes of work. This type of sheet can also be used to record the use of ICT in the curriculum in addition to a taught IT course.

Recording work done by individual pupils

Pupil records may be kept in the form of a diary, in which the pupil records the IT s/he has done in each lesson every day. The **advantages** of this approach are that:

■ pupils complete the diary themselves, which means less paperwork for you;
■ looking through the diaries on, say, a fortnightly or monthly basis will give you a good idea of the quantity and quality of IT the pupils are enjoying.

The **disadvantages** of this approach are that:

■ it is difficult or time-consuming to collate the data contained in the diaries;
■ pupils may lose their diaries;
■ if you keep the diaries for the pupils, storage space may be an issue, and the immediacy of using the diary may be lost.

An alternative approach is to keep a record sheet for each pupil, on which the teacher ticks and initials the relevant boxes when the pupil has completed a particular piece of work.

IT Order (KS3)	Unit or Activity	English	Maths	Science	MFL	Geog	History	D&T
1a	U3	• Sept /			• Jan			
1b	U2							
1c	U6							• Dec/Jan
1d	U1		• Oct					
1e	U7			• Nov				
1f	U4			• Apr				
2a	U5	• Sep						
2b	U8	•	•	•	•	•	•	•
2c	U9						• Mar	
2d	U10					• Feb		

Figure 7.2 – Example of a record sheet for IT work covered

This approach has the **advantages** that:

- you have only one sheet per pupil;
- you can see at a glance how much work the pupil has done.

It has the following **disadvantages**, however:

- The use of such a sheet can encourage pupils to aim to have as much of the sheet as possible ticked, rather than concentrating on understanding the concepts and skills being taught.
- Storage can be a problem.
- It is still difficult to collate the information.

One way of overcoming the last disadvantage is to create a database or spreadsheet to record the work that pupils have completed. Using a spreadsheet, for example, it is possible to insert formulae that will count how many Units a pupil has completed, and to show you this information at a glance. It is time-consuming setting this up, but this is a one-off cost because you can use the same basic spreadsheet, with different pupil names, for years to come.

You may find it hard to persuade staff to enter the information. A possible solution is to make pupils or students responsible for doing so. They are usually honest! Of course, this will not be feasible where pupils are very young or where access to computers is an issue.

A third type of record sheet is a front cover sheet for each individual Unit or piece of work done. This can provide spaces for the teacher to comment on the work, and to set further targets for the pupil. This has the following **advantages**:

- It encourages staff to write comments rather than just tick the work or give it a mark.
- It can provide useful feedback to the pupil.

But it has the following **disadvantages**:

- The forms are time-consuming to complete.
- Again, it is difficult to collate the information for individual pupils and classes or year groups.

Recording extra-curricular IT work

Many pupils and students do work on computers at home and in clubs or summer schools and the like. Print-outs resulting from this activity are not very good as evidence of achievement in themselves, because they were produced in an unstructured situation and the context may not be known to you. (See the section on judging pupils' IT capability by the finished product, on page 97.) However, they may be useful as supporting evidence, especially if pupils and students are asked to complete a front sheet that indicates the nature of the task undertaken and how much assistance was given.

One final point about record-keeping: it needs to be said that you do not need to keep reams of print-outs as evidence of pupils' work. The comments in your mark book are just as much evidence as print-outs.

However, especially where IT is delivered across the curriculum, you would find it useful to keep representative samples of pupils' work. It is also useful to have an assurance that, should you need to look at their work done in other classes, it will be made available to you.

Managing the assessment of IT

We are concerned here with the management of assessment rather than assessment itself.

Assessing IT capability presents a problem for teachers for one or more of the following reasons:

- The Level descriptors in the IT Programme of Study appear to be vague.
- Different teachers have different views on what constitutes a high level of IT capability.

- Pupils' IT capability cannot be judged solely by looking at the finished product.
- Staff do not always know enough about IT themselves to be able to accurately evaluate the IT work done by others.

Let's examine each of these in turn, along with possible solutions.

The Level descriptors seem vague

Assessment is not an exact science, and so any attempt to define IT capability in a meaningful way is bound to appear vague to some extent. The alternative would be to have a very structured skills-based approach, but the problem there is that it is easier to assess low level tasks rather than higher level ones.

To a large extent, whether a student has achieved Level 5 or Level 6 will be a matter for you and other colleagues to decide. It is important to realise that a pupil does not have to have attained every item in a Level descriptor to be said to be at that Level – in fact, s/he may not have attained everything in that 'slot', but may have done some of the things described in the Level above.

Also, the Level descriptors are not intended to be broken down into component parts, and hence a tick list. This was the approach encouraged, perhaps inadvertently, by the previous IT Programme of Study.

You and other IT teachers can get to grips with the Level descriptors by:

- reading and discussing the exemplification materials provided by SCAA (now the QCA);
- summarising the Level descriptors for non-specialist staff and pupils;
- attending relevant INSET courses run by your LEA;
- discussing the issues with other IT Co-ordinators at conferences organised by IT organisations or through mailing lists and news groups (see Appendix);
- reading the educational IT periodicals (see Appendix).

Differences of opinion about what constitutes IT capability

This, too, requires discussion and moderation. This issue is especially problematic where the IT Programme of Study is delivered through other subjects, because what may be complicated in terms of the other subject may not be so in terms of IT.

As a case in point, a pentagon is a more complex figure in mathematical terms than a square. However, in terms of LOGO programming, the same skills and understanding are involved in making the turtle draw a pentagon as in drawing a square.

This kind of situation can give rise to low level tasks being set, and pupils being given more credit than they truly deserve.

Even amongst IT experts, the issue still arises. For example, is a pupil who uses a 'wizard' to create a newsletter showing greater or lesser IT capability than a pupil who doesn't use a 'wizard'?

To overcome the problem of differences of opinion, it would be useful to:

- distinguish between skills, such as drawing text frames, and understanding, shown by, for example, designing a newsletter with a particular audience in mind;
- discuss the issue with colleagues, and decide the issue in the form of a policy, or as part of the ICT policy.

Judging pupils' IT capability by the finished product

Because of the existence of 'wizards', and easy access to data and information via the internet or CD-ROMs, it is simply impossible to judge a pupil's level of IT capability only from their printed work. Even if the work has spelling errors, say, this may reflect their inability to read well rather than a lack of awareness of the benefits of using a spell checker.

A print-out cannot tell you, for example, if the pupil centred the heading by using the spacebar or the proper tool provided by the software.

To assess pupils' IT capability:

- you have to observe what s/he does;
- you have to make sure other staff know what sorts of things to look out for;
- ask pupils working on spreadsheets to print out the sheet showing the formulae used (and observe them using and copying the formulae);

- ask pupils to complete a self-assessment sheet, or state why and how they did a particular thing, because this provides you with additional information that you can use to inform your assessment decisions.

Lack of staff expertise in IT

There is a limit to how far you can support non-expert staff by adopting a sort of 'painting by numbers' approach to the teaching and assessment of IT. You need to:

- ideally, persuade the senior management team that IT should be taught by experts;
- if this is not possible, or if IT is to be taught by everyone, you will need to raise their expertise by running or buying in INSET, or recommending courses for staff. See Chapter 12 for further information on INSET.

It is important to ensure that the tasks set give pupils the opportunity to demonstrate what they know, understand and can do. If staff do not know what is possible in IT, the tasks they set will tend to be closed. The more open-ended a task is, the harder it is to assess – but the richer the opportunity it provides for pupils to excel.

Chapter 8
The infrastructure

The options

The problem

You will not be surprised to learn that the options for hardware are changing all the time. As far as possible, you should attempt to maximise your options. This does not mean not coming to no decision at all, but it does mean trying not to put all your eggs in one basket.

For example, if you are starting an infrastructure project that will take two or three years to complete, don't rush out and buy all the hardware now. Like software, hardware tends to fall in price and increase in specifications very rapidly – and every so often the technical specifications and requirements change completely.

This book is not meant to be a technical manual, and even if it were it would be out of date by the time you bought it. What this chapter does is to provide you with criteria for evaluating different types of solution.

The word 'solution' implies the existence of a problem. The problem can be thought of as a series of inter-related questions:

- How can we ensure computer access to as many people as possible?
- How can we ensure that the infrastructure can be adapted or used for different types of user, with changing needs?
- How can we ensure that the system is modern, and able to be kept modern?
- How can we ensure that the system is manageable?
- How can we achieve all this without going bankrupt?

The solution

Not all of these questions can be answered technically. In fact, ultimately all of these questions are management issues which are affected by technical matters and/or financial matters.

In this chapter we consider three main types of solution:

- networks;
- stand-alone computers;
- portable options.

Networks

Generally speaking, a network is an arrangement in which computers are linked to each other. Someone using one computer or workstation on the network is able to see files on another computer on the network, if s/he has permission to do so and the network has been set up to allow it.

The **advantages** of networks are that:

- they are easier to maintain than stand-alones, because you can do many things in one go, and from one computer;
- it is easier to set up standard installations on every computer;
- users can gain access to their work from any workstation on the network;
- users can have access to different printers and other resources without moving from their seat;

- any templates and other utilities that one user creates can be made available to all other users very quickly;
- you can make software and work available to all pupils and pupils very quickly and easily;
- networks are often more secure than stand-alone machines.

The **disadvantages** of networks are that:

- they can cause inconvenience to anyone not yet recognised as a user;
- some software doesn't work across a network;
- if the network server 'goes down' or, on some types of network, if one of the workstations stops working, the whole network can stop;
- setting up and maintaining a network can be quite demanding of technical expertise;
- networks are more expensive to set up than stand-alones because of the need to put in the infrastructure such as cabling.

The picture can be summarised by stating that networks are expensive and complicated to set up, but very easy to use and run – especially now that you can buy in a managed service (see Chapter 9). On the other hand, stand-alone computers are easy to set up, but time-consuming to maintain, and not very convenient when dealing with classes of more than, say, 7 or 8 pupils.

Types of network

There are two main kinds of network:

- peer-to-peer networks;
- client-server networks.

A peer-to-peer network is one in which computers are linked to each other via a cable or infra-red radiation. It is effectively a means of sharing resources such as a printer.

The **advantages** of the peer-to-peer network are:

- it is very easy to set up;
- it is inexpensive to set up;

- it requires little more expertise to maintain than does a stand-alone system;
- it can save money by making a printer and other resources available to more than one computer.

The **disadvantages** of this type of network are that:

- it is only really suitable for a handful of computers (about 10), and so would be fine in a small office but not for pupil use in most circumstances;
- it is not as fast as client-server networks;
- generally speaking, it does not have the same security features as a client-server network.

A client-server network is one in which several workstations (clients) are provided with software and other services via a fileserver.

The advantages and disadvantages of this type of network are the inverse of those of the peer-to-peer network. In addition, client-server networks can be relatively inexpensive to expand, because you can plan to use thin clients or older computers.

Thin clients are workstations which do not store any data themselves, but get everything from the file server. In addition, there are some network solutions which enable you to put virtually any computer onto the network.

There are, of course, other variations, such as networks which use web workstations, designed to give easy access to the internet.

Planning the network

When planning a new network or upgrading an existing one, it is a good idea to ask several companies to demonstrate their wares, if this is practicable, and to give you a quotation. In many LEAs you have to go out to tender to several companies if the cost is above a certain level.

You will have to consider whether the same company should supply the computers, software and infrastructure. This can be the more expensive option, but on the other hand there is only one company to deal with if anything goes wrong. (See the section on managed services in Chapter 9.)

Questions to ask the cabling company include:

- Will the cable carry the signal from the server to the furthest point on the network, or will a device called a hub be required?
- If two buildings are to be networked, is the best method to use physical cabling or wireless technology?
- How much disruption will be caused by drilling etc? Can the work be scheduled to be carried out during the holidays?
- Will the company provide a method statement? This is a document which sets out exactly what they will do, and when they will complete each stage by.
- Does the company have a named representative who takes responsibility for health and safety issues?

Other factors that need to be considered are:

- Can the cabling be hidden, so that it is not vulnerable to vandalism?
- Have all parties who are likely to be affected by building works been informed of what is going on (see 'Who to inform', page 105)?

Questions to ask the potential suppliers of the network include:

- Is training provided as part of the package? If so, what sort of training, and how much?
- What software is supplied?
- How many servers will be needed for the size of your network? (Be careful of answers which seem too good to be true.)
- Does the network come with network management software (see Chapter 3)? If so, has it been designed by the company, or is it, at the other extreme, a collection of shareware utilities?
- How easy is it to set up CD-ROMs to run over the network? Once set up, how easy is it for users to select from a menu of titles?
- How fast do multimedia applications run over the network?
- What support is provided as part of the package? What extra support can you buy?
- What is the nature of the support? For example, is telephone

support included? Does the company provide remote diagnosis and fixing (ie via a modem connected to the server)? Does the company provide a complete managed service? (See Chapter 9.)

■ Can the company provide you with details of three reference sites, ie schools or colleges similar to yours that are using their network?

This is not an exhaustive list, but it does give you a good idea of the sorts of questions you need to have answered before you have the network installed.

When comparing different suppliers' answers, you should:

■ mark their answers on a grid prepared for the purpose;

■ not be swayed by claims which seem to good to be true;

■ consider using weighting to reflect the relative importance to you of different questions;

■ consider ways to deal with answers which are not directly comparable (eg, one company may be more expensive than another, but provide a faster response time when you ask for technical assistance).

You will also need to ask a number of questions internally, such as:

■ How much disruption to courses will be caused while the network is being installed?

■ How can any disruption be minimised, in terms of lesson content and delivery?

■ Will the network be distributed around the building, or concentrated in one or two rooms, or a combination of both? (See the section on distribution of resources in Chapter 4.) Note that it is a good idea to place data points in rooms even if you do not yet have the computers to plug into them, unless wireless technology is used, because it is usually cheaper to do all the cabling in one go. It is not, however, necessarily a good idea to buy more hubs than you need because by the time you do need them you will probably find that the technology has improved and that the price has gone down.

■ How many printers will there be, where will they be located, and who will have access to what?

- Will curriculum users have access to administrative modules such as attendance and timetables? Giving staff access can save a lot of time. (See Chapter 10.)
- How many computers will be set up in the staffroom(s)? If none, will there be a staff resources area where staff can work away from pupils?
- Will computers be placed in the library?
- Where will scanners be located?
- Who will manage the network?

Even the smallest network is quite a large commitment in terms of all the strands involved – planning, decisions regarding the technology to be used, choosing the right company or companies, cabling, installation, setting up, and minimising the disruption to all users of the facilities.

For the project to be successful you must liaise with all parties concerned in order to make sure that the network is delivered on time and within budget. One of the most important aspects of successful project management is keeping people informed.

Who to inform

The people you need to tell what is happening, and when, could include:

- the senior management team;
- the teaching staff;
- the network manager;
- other administrative staff;
- the caretaker(s);
- other ancillary staff;
- parents;
- community groups;
- youth clubs;
- literacy schools;
- adult day and evening courses;
- local businesses if they use the facilities in the evenings;

- sports associations;
- church choir, amateur operatic or drama clubs and so on.

It is a good idea to inform people in writing whenever possible, in case they forget or are off sick at a critical time. Even if you tell them informally, you should follow it up with a fax, letter or email.

Stand-alone systems

These are much easier and quicker to set up than networks, but can pose immense management problems. Even having just two or three stand-alone computers in a school or college can cause inconvenience in terms of trouble-shooting, because you cannot fix problems from another workstation. Monitoring computer usage for copyright breaches, or simply in order to find out how it is being used, is not easy. Nor are antivirus measures easy to maintain. Have a look at the tasks listed in Chapter 5 as well.

However, there may be a good reason to have some stand-alone systems. Good reasons might include the following:

- Some software may work faster on a stand-alone system. For example, you want to set up a multimedia workstation. On some networks, the only way you could allow users to access the computer's actual CD-ROM drive would be to give them some administrator privileges, which it would not be wise to do.
- In older buildings, it may be physically impossible, or prohibitively expensive, for some classrooms or offices to be connected to the network. Ultimately, it would probably be less bother in the long run to move the incumbent of the office to a better location.
- Rather than throw older equipment out, it may be possible to use them in particular locations and/or for certain purposes.

Portable options

There is much that can be done with a bit of imagination. Portable computers and other peripherals (such as digital cameras) can be an extremely useful addition to your ICT resources, although they can be difficult to manage, especially if they are the sole resource.

Examples of portable solutions include:

- *palmtop computers*, which are relatively inexpensive, can easily be taken out on school trips and whose small keys are well-suited to younger children's hands;

- *quasi-computers*, which have word processing, and sometimes spreadsheet and other software; these are not as expensive as laptops, and have bigger screens and keys than palmtops, and have been popular with teachers working with children with special educational needs;

- *laptops*, which provide all the processing power of their larger cousins but are expensive to buy and become outdated very quickly; also, the more powerful they are, the less time the battery lasts, generally speaking.

When considering portable solutions, you need to ask yourself questions like:

How long can they be used away from a mains source? Note that manufacturers' stated times often refer to how long the computer will run on battery if it is switched on and then not used. The more you access the drives, especially the CD-ROM and floppy drives, the shorter the time it will last.

- Where will they be stored, taking into account security considerations?
- On what basis will the equipment be used or lent out?
- How will you try to ensure that software is not installed or deleted without your authorisation, and how will you put matters right if it is?
- How will pupils print their work?
- Can the computers be linked to your network, or to other computers, to transfer files or to print work?

While considering the right solution for your school or college, bear in mind that:

- every option has its management advantages and disadvantages;
- no technical solution is of any use unless it is referenced to the

curriculum and the way people actually work in your institution;
- there are many possibilities.

Project management

Whatever the type of infrastructure is decided upon, or whatever the nature of the improvements being made, you need to make sure that certain rules of project management are adhered to:

- Draw up a timetable indicating what should have happened, by when, and who is responsible.

- Make sure everyone concerned is kept informed – especially when something goes wrong.

- Keep a close eye on expenditure – but also find out how flexible your budget constraints are.

- Don't forget to allow for 'hidden' costs such as delivery charges.

- Try to hold some money in reserve for contingency purposes – but check whether you will lose it if you don't spend it all by the end of the financial year.

- When purchasing goods and services, allow enough time for the companies to invoice you, and for you to check deliveries before authorising payment.

- When dealing with companies, ask to deal with a named representative all the time rather than several people.

- Keep an up-to-date record of what has gone on, and make this accessible to others just in case you are off work through illness at a critical time.

- Make sure your filing system is logical and systematic, so that anyone can locate files in your absence.

Chapter 9
Financial management

Introduction

Financial management cannot be truly efficient unless it is linked to aims and objectives. These should be set out in your ICT Policy and ICT Strategy, as explained in Chapter 2.

There are three main aspects of financial management:

- investment planning;
- purchasing;
- capitation management.

Investment planning

Replacing and updating equipment

Generally speaking, five years is held to be the time limit on the life of a computer. This is really just an accounting figure. Computers obviously don't stop being functional when they are just over 5 years old, and if you really want to keep up to date you should replace equipment after a few months.

As technology progresses, expectations change, and this is reflected in schemes of work and pupils' and staff attitudes towards equipment (and software). Thus, even if your computers are working perfectly, if they look old-fashioned, and/or the software on them does not have the functionality that people have come to expect, many people will be put off using them. On the other hand, some teachers want to keep them, and feel comfortable with them.

The Stevenson Report 'Information and Communications Technology in UK Schools: An Independent Enquiry' (available from

http://rubble.ultralab.anglia.ac.uk/stevenson/contents.html)

said the Government should 'make sure that no hardware equipment over 5 years old is included in any official counts to avoid a false sense of complacency', and this seems to be as good a yardstick as any.

In simplistic terms, if you adopt 5 years as the benchmark, you need to make sure that 20% of the equipment is replaced each year, so that by the end of 5 years all of the equipment will have been replaced. This is an ongoing process.

Unfortunately, real life is not quite as simple as that, mainly due to two factors:

- Unless your school has already reached what it considers to be an ideal ratio of computers to pupils, with the right number of printers and other facilities, you will almost certainly want to increase the amount of hardware, not merely replace it.

- If you purchase all of your equipment in one go, it will all become 5 years old at the same time – a major issue when equipment has been donated to the school or acquired through a bid or special project.

The second factor does not get around the need for an investment plan, it means that the school or college may have to be more creative about how it implements it. For example, it may be possible to save the money in a special account, or it could go for a leasing arrangement (see below). Your job is to work out how much must be put aside or spent each year to maintain the desired standard of provision, and then make your case.

By investment plan is meant a commitment on the part of the school or college to ensure that when equipment becomes obsolete (defined as over 5 years old), equipment has been purchased to replace it.

There are two types of 'plan' which should be avoided if at all possible. These are:

- The 'plan' adopted by many schools, of 'crossing that bridge when we come to it', does not enable the ICT manager to plan very far ahead, and so makes implementation of an ICT Strategy something of a hit and miss affair.
- Financing by 'windfall', in which the Head or Principal finds money each year to spend on ICT, is not much good either, unless it is in addition to a regular amount of funding each year. It is impossible to plan ahead if you don't know how much, if anything, you are going to receive. It also means that when you do receive money, you may be tempted to spend it quickly in case it 'disappears' – a problem that is less likely to arise if a special ICT replacement or investment fund has been set up.

Having said that, it is a good idea to maintain a 'shopping list' of items that you would buy if you had the money. If the Head offers you £500 to be spent (or at least committed) by tomorrow, what would you buy? What if s/he offered you £5000 on the same conditions?

Managing different versions of software

Software also needs to be updated for reasons given earlier, and is often updated automatically when you purchase new equipment. For example, when you buy new PCs, they almost always come with the latest version of Windows.

The problem you face here is managing different software versions. Ideally, if someone produces work in one part of the site, they should be able to edit it in another part of the site. Put another way, they should be able to complete work on one computer that they started on another computer. As a rule, work produced in the latest version of a program cannot be edited in previous versions.

There are several ways to manage software upgrades:

■ Upgrade all software at the same time. This is the least problematic option in some respects, but is also the most expensive, and can be the most time-consuming if you mainly use stand-alones. You will also have to consider how to keep disruption to a minimum, and what staff training issues are involved.

■ Upgrade certain computers or computer rooms only. For example, you may decide to upgrade only the computers used by Year 6 classes, or the IT GCSE class.

■ Upgrade staff computers first, so that staff become familiar with the new software before using it in their classes. Note, however, that this can cause confusion, because it is easy to forget that what you did in the staffroom cannot be reproduced in the classroom because of the different software versions being used.

■ Have a policy of not upgrading the oldest computers. This makes sense when the older computers do not have enough processing power to run the latest version of the software. There will usually be subject teachers who can make good use of a computer with older software.

Perhaps it should be said that software should only be updated if the newer version offers clear advantages, and even then not until the bugs have been ironed out.

Generally speaking, software development goes through the following stages:

1 *Alpha*. This is the equivalent of a first draft of a document, with many bugs and/or unfinished parts.

2 *Technical beta*. This looks like the final version will look, but intended for internal use only.

3 *Marketing beta*. This is almost finished, but may have a few bugs or unfinished features, or be in plain packaging or have no manual.

4 *First release*.

Unfortunately, the first release is not always bug-free, and it is often worth waiting a few months for the next release before buying.

Whenever you have a situation in which not all computers have the same versions of the software, there are two main strategies you can adopt. These are not mutually exclusive.

- Set up the new software to save files in the old format. This may entail some loss of functionality, but this shouldn't really matter, because the user is usually able to override the default settings. If you use programs like Microsoft Office, consider purchasing the Resource Kit, or ask your LEA about it. The Resource Kit contains policy templates which enable you very quickly to set up a standard installation on all machines, governing such things as the format in which files are saved, and where they are saved.

- If one is available, install a utility which will enable users of the older software to read and print documents files created in the latest version. A more sophisticated version of this is to set up an intranet, if it is technically feasible and if financial resources allow.

Making use of older equipment

As stated earlier, older equipment does not suddenly stop working when it becomes 5 years old. Here are some considerations to bear in mind when deciding how to distribute resources and what to do with older equipment:

- It is a good idea to install the most up to date equipment in areas where they are going to be used in the teaching of IT, in order to ensure that the equipment will be fully used, both in terms of how much it is used, and what it is used for.

- In classrooms where there is one computer, installing a newer one should mean that there are now two computers. From an IT perspective, it doesn't matter too much whether children use, say, an Acorn program for research or word processing, or a PC program, as long as children using the older equipment are not disadvantaged.

- The older equipment may be able to be used in particular areas or for particular purposes. For example, it may be worthwhile setting up a computer to act as a print server on a network. Its sole purpose would be to store documents which are in the queue for printing, but in some circumstances this could speed up printing tremendously.

- In a secondary school or college, older computers can often be used for specialist purposes in departments. For example, a computer with data logging and spreadsheet software could be located permanently in one of the science labs, or a computer containing a high specification painting program could be set up in an art room.
- Staff with their own offices may even want to use them for their own administration.
- If push comes to shove, you can probably sell them, or give them away to a charity. The skip really should be a last resort.

Having said that, there are certain disadvantages of using older equipment:

- The equipment may look tatty. This can have a negative effect on the way pupils treat the equipment, and may lack visual appeal for OFSTED inspectors and other visitors.
- Users of the equipment may be left further and further behind other teachers and pupils in terms of what they can achieve with computers.
- Governors and members of the senior management team, seeing rooms brimming with computers, may decide that large scale investment is not immediately necessary after all.

Investment plan checklist

When working on the ICT investment plan, make sure you take into account the following factors – or, at least, those which apply to your circumstances:

- Projected pupil numbers.
- Courses or schemes of work planned over the next few years – these plans will almost certainly affect hardware and software requirements.
- Planned (extra) computer rooms, if applicable.
- Fileservers. Generally speaking, fileservers can handle about 80 workstations efficiently, so if you have a network of 100 computers or more, you should think about budgeting for 2 fileservers.

- Hubs.
- Repeaters.
- Cabling.
- Other infrastructure. (If building work is necessary, find out if that comes under a different budget.)
- Workstations.
- Software licences.
- Printers.
- Scanners.
- Digital cameras.
- Palmtop computers.
- Laptop computers.
- Other portable computers or quasi-computers.
- Ad hoc allowance for new hardware.
- Software licences.
- New software titles.

Purchasing

Ways of paying for hardware

Financing an ICT investment plan can be a huge undertaking. There are several ways of buying the equipment:

- *Paying for it straight away.* This has the advantage of giving you the flexibility of buying from the company which is giving the best deal at the time (subject to compatibility considerations). The main disadvantage is that it may not be possible to buy new equipment when you need it, if the funds are not available.

- *Lease purchasing.* This entails having the equipment now, but paying for it over several years – in other words it is a loan. It may be possible to take ownership of the equipment at the end of the loan term, assuming you would want to take ownership of old equipment, and also assuming you were able to avoid acting illegally: schools are not legally able to own the equipment. The advantage of this approach is that you get the equipment now even if you cannot afford it. The disadvantages are being tied in to one supplier and having to pay interest charges.

■ *Lease hiring*. This is a form of hiring the equipment instead of buying it. In some types of agreement you have an option to upgrade the equipment every so often. This approach therefore has the advantage of addressing the problem of replacing obsolete equipment, while the disadvantages are, again, being tied to one supplier and interest charges..

See the Appendix for more information on these options.

Preferred suppliers policy?

Find out if your LEA or Governing Body operates a preferred suppliers policy for certain products. If it is compulsory for you to make purchases from a particular supplier there is no point in wasting time looking at alternative suppliers' prices.

However, the preferred suppliers policy may apply only below a certain threshold of expenditure.

You may even wish to institute your own preferred suppliers policy. Purchasing from one company enables you to build up a relationship which may enable you to benefit from special prices and discounts.

The main disadvantages of a preferred suppliers policy are potentially higher prices being charged, and poor customer service because of the lack of a competitive edge.

One option favoured by several LEAs and schools is to have a renewable preferred suppliers policy. Tenders are invited, and the winning company becomes the preferred supplier for 2 or 3 years.

Inviting tenders

Much of this area has already been covered in the section entitled Planning the network, in Chapter 8. Before embarking on this course your school or college should seek specialist advice, but in general the steps you need to take are as follows:

      1   Decide what it is you are hoping to purchase, for example, a network comprising a fileserver, a hub, and

50 workstations, or specify what you want to achieve in terms of access, speed and software.

2   Advertise in the press (which may include newspapers from all over Europe, not just the UK).

3   Set out the specification in printed form.

4   From the tenders that arrive by the deadline you have specified, select three or four that appear to meet your criteria.

5   Invite those companies to demonstrate their product and answer your questions. (This may not always be practicable, in which case obtain quotations and product specifications only.)

6   Take a decision on which company, if any, wins the contract.

The tendering process also encompasses other factors, including the following:

■ The process must be seen to be fair. That means asking all of the companies the same main questions, although realistically your follow-up questions may differ as you respond to different answers to the main questions.

■ The process should be confidential. The companies involved should not be given details of what the other companies have proposed, since that could give them an unfair advantage.

■ The result must be justifiable. If one of the companies that fails to win the contract demands to know why not, you have to be able to justify your decision without breaking the confidentiality rule. This should not be a problem if you adopt the points system described next.

It is difficult to be completely objective, but you should strive to be as objective as possible. One way of doing so is to adopt a points system. This means assigning points to each question, up to a maximum number of points per question.

The points system should also include an element of weighting, to reflect your priorities.

For example, if technical support is less important than price, assign a greater number of points to the costs than to the technical support options.

Technical support

It is clearly very important to consider what technical support is available when you purchase your hardware. In many cases there is a basic support package which you can upgrade straight away. The kind of options available to you include:

- unlimited telephone support;
- X number of days training;
- on-site repairs;
- return to base repairs;
- 4 working hour response time;
- 8 working hour response time;
- remote problem-solving via modem;
- managed services (see below).

See the Appendix for further information on managed services.

Managed services provide individual schools or LEAs, or even clusters of schools or LEAs with what is effectively a 'one-stop shop' in which the school buys the hardware, software and technical support from one company.

This has two main **advantages**, these being:

- You are dealing with one company for everything, so you should not have to contend with the problem of hardware people blaming the software, or the software people blaming the hardware, when something goes wrong.
- It can be a cost-effective solution to the problem of finding and then employing a technician, since many problems can be solved remotely via a modem as a result of a telephone call to report the problem.

The main **disadvantage** of using managed services is that you are tied to a particular company for some time.

Capitation

Most ICT managers obtain most of their funding from the school or college budget, sometimes in the form of an annual capitation allowance. This should be seen as a separate issue from investment plan funding. The latter is for capital spending, such as hardware and infrastructure, while capitation is mainly for current spending, such as consumables.

Factors which should affect the amount of the allowance

You may simply be given an amount of money, or you may have to bid for it. Either way, you should ask for several matters to be considered:

- Has a distinction been drawn between the spending requirements arising directly from the teaching of IT, and those arising from the use of ICT in other subjects? Put starkly, will you be responsible for replacing the laser printer toner used by the English department? If so, your capitation allowance should reflect this. (If not, who **will** pay for it, and what will be the payment mechanism involved? If pencils, say, are purchased from a central fund, should not toner cartridges etc be also?)

- Has the number of pupils been taken into account?

- Have new courses been taken into account? A new GCSE course, for example, will, you hope, attract more pupils.

- Has the number of (keen) staff been taken into account? More use equals more expense.

- Have expansion plans been taken into account? If ICT is well-managed, increasing the availability of computers and printers increases the demand for printing.

- Has non-computer work been taken into account? See the section on spending decisions below for further advice on this.

Bidding for funds

If you are invited to put in a bid for your allowance, and there is no formal bidding process in place, it may be helpful to carry out the following process:

- Address the questions listed in the foregoing section.
- Relate your spending plans to your ICT strategy (see chapter 2).
- Be specific, not vague.
- Keep your bid to one side of A4.

Spending decisions

When drawing up spending plans for the next financial year, you will need to take into account some or all of the following:

- the fact that the academic year and the financial year start and finish at different times: you do not want to run out of funds in July;
- the requirements of the IT (and other?) schemes of work, in terms of software for example;
- blank diskettes, CD-ROMs, backup tapes;
- non-computer based work, which requires plain and lined paper, exercise books, crayons etc;
- miscellaneous stationery items such as Sellotape, stapler and staples, hole punch;
- boxes of pens and pencils for lending out to pupils;
- filing requirements, such as filing cabinets, box files, ring binders;
- teacher tools, such as mark books, merit certificates, board markers, smiley face stamps;
- photocopying and related requirements: estimate this by reference to your scheme of work, but allow for wastage and for unplanned worksheets;
- delivery charges and, in some circumstances, VAT;
- the probable need to replenish supplies of toner cartridges and other consumables throughout the year;
- the fact that it is a good idea to add a contingency allowance of, say, 5% of the total.

Book-keeping

Meticulous book-keeping is the key to financial planning. Whether you use a paper system, a computerised system or a mixture of the two, your records should be able to inform you:

- when the items on each invoice were delivered;
- when each invoice was paid;
- how much money you had to start with;
- how much money is left;
- how much money has been spent in the past financial year on each of various categories, such as photocopying, software, stationery etc.

Needless to say, your book-keeping system should also be closely related to your stock checking and inventory systems. See Chapter 5 for advice in that area.

Keeping accounts like this will assist you in making informed decisions about future spending plans which are based in part on your planned and actual spending in the previous financial year.

Other sources of funds

Although the capitation allowance is the main source of funding for IT, it is not the only one. Public and private money is available, quite often for specific projects. Also, it may be possible to obtain sponsorship from a local company, perhaps in the form of one or more computer systems. See the Appendix for further details of sources of funds.

Chapter 10
Managing the paperwork

Useful concepts and ideas for deling with administrative tasks

Good practice

There are several general ideas you should know about in order to ensure good practice, not only by yourself or those staff who teach IT, but across the board. Good practice means:

- not having to retype data, ie getting it right first time;
- not losing documents;
- not having to redesign documents unnecessarily.

There are several concepts you should know about, and tell others about. These are:

- efficient data transfer;
- templates;
- automatic processing;
- linking documents;

■ mail-merging.

Efficient data transfer

Data can be transferred from one application to another in a variety of ways, such as via the clipboard (by copying and pasting), or by exporting and importing. You may need to save your file in TSV or CSV format first (see below). In a nutshell, if you have data in a file, you should be able to put that data into any other kind of file, be it a word processed document, a spreadsheet, a database or anything else. It should even be possible to transfer data between different types of computer, different operating systems and different types of program.

One obvious way of achieving this kind of mobility of data is to set up an intranet, if you have a network. An intranet has the same qualities as the internet, the most important one in the present context being the fact that anyone can access any data if it is converted to HTML format and every workstation has a web browser. If, however, you do not have an intranet set up, you can still fall back on the other techniques mentioned, such as converting databases to tab or comma separated values.

Tab-separated values are where fields, such as name, form, subject etc, are separated by pressing the TAB key.

Note that you should separate each field by one tab only: don't try to line the text up by pressing the TAB key several times.

Comma-separated values are where fields are separated by commas.

Note that you should not separate fields by pressing the space bar. Sometimes fields are enclosed in quotation marks. Records are usually separated by the Return or Enter character (¶).

Templates

A template is a document that contains text and formatting information. If you base all documents (of whatever type) on a template, you will not have to keep entering the same text or designing the document anew each time. The pages in this book were created from a template, which is why they all have the same general appearance.

Templates have a number of advantages, including the following:

- They help to create a sense of corporate identity, because all documents of a particular type look similar (which can help with marketing too – see Chapter 11).
- They can help to reduce formatting and spelling errors.
- They save people from having to worry about formatting issues, thereby freeing them to get on with the job in hand.
- In some circumstances, for example a lesson plan template, they can act as a prompt to remind you of what to address in the document.

The kinds of template you can set up include ones for:

- schemes of work;
- unit planning;
- lesson planning;
- stationery, such as a memorandum;
- cover work for absence known in advance;
- class register;
- merit certificate;
- stock control;
- electronic mark book.

Automatic processing

Wherever possible, use either macros (small programs that can carry out tedious or time-consuming tasks) or fields, which are variables that contain data that changes, such as the number of pages in a document.

A macro could reduce a two hour task to a few seconds. The more sophisticated or ambitious the macro, the longer it will take to trouble-shoot. When creating a macro, it is a good idea to:

- draw up a flow chart of what the macro is designed to achieve;
- add to the flow chart branches arising from 'if' statements;
- record the actions to be undertaken by the macro where possible, as this will save time;

- annotate the macro or keep notes on what each part of it is doing'
- build in error-checking;
- test it as thoroughly as possible;
- test it on non-critical data;
- test it at a non-critical time;
- write instructions on how to use it;
- get someone else to test it;
- include its version number in the comments section and in any documentation you produce to accompany it.

Linking documents

It is possible to insert figures from a spreadsheet into a word-processed document in such a way that whenever you change the spreadsheet the document is also changed automatically. Look in the program's on-line Help for Object Linking and Embedding, or Paste-Special.

This is a very useful technique to use where the same data appears in several documents. For example, suppose you have prepared reports for parents, other staff and the Governing Body on how much has been spent on ICT over the last year. Although the reports will be written differently, they will use the same spreadsheet data. If you embed the spreadsheet data in each document, any changes you make to the data will automatically be reflected in the documents which are linked to it.

Incidentally, this is a good example of why it is money well spent to buy software that contains advanced features, rather than cheaper software that does not have the same degree of functionality.

Mail-merging

This is the process whereby data which changes is merged with data which doesn't. For example, you can issue certificates of achievement which automatically contain the pupil's name, and what modules s/he has excelled in.

Many of the techniques described above can be combined. For example, it is possible to create a template which contains macros that run automatically when you create a new document based on it. The macro might prompt the user for a file name, and then save the document in a special folder.

Here is another example. You could set up a spreadsheet containing pupils' names and their test results. If several people teach IT, they can each be asked to enter the marks for their own classes. The spreadsheet could be set up to translate the marks into a level, and a device called a lookup table could be used to describe what each level means. You could then set up a separate word processed certificate template linked to the spreadsheet. When all the test results have been entered into the spreadsheet, carry out the mail-merge to produce a stack of individual certificates each containing:

- the pupil's name;
- the pupil's test result;
- the pupil's level;
- a description of what the level means.

You can also use mail-merge to produce labels for exercise books and other items. This can be especially useful in the primary school.

Note that using mail-merge to produce labels for pupil helpers and staff to wear can be very impressive, and can therefore help to promote a positive image of IT and ICT.

Administration-reducing checklist

Whatever the situation that prevails where you work, there is much you can do to reduce the administrative burden on yourself and your colleagues. Remember that helping others to reduce their workload could be good from a public relations perspective! Here is a list of things you can do, some of which have been mentioned earlier:

- Use a computer for producing documents, even where it seems not worthwhile doing so, so that work can be updated easily.

- Use templates and the other time-saving techniques described in the previous section.

- Make pupil data available on disk, network or intranet.

- Make policies, lesson plans and other documentation available on disk, network or intranet.

- Set up a spreadsheet for analysing and predicting grades (where appropriate).

- Ask colleagues only for data that you really need.

What the DfEE is doing

This section is for your information only – you don't have to actually do anything!

The DfEE Working Group

Teachers have naturally always been concerned with raising standards of achievement. However, as the drive to raise standards is more and more relentlessly pursued under the auspices of various initiatives, it is perhaps inevitable that the administrative burden on teachers has increased accordingly.

There are several questions which arise:

- Are all of the tasks teachers are asked to undertake necessary in order to raise achievement?

- If the tasks *are* necessary, do *teachers* need to undertake them?

- If teachers *do* need to undertake them, can the tasks be done more efficiently using computers?

This is a situation which has not escaped the notice of the Government itself. In 1998, the DfEE established a Working Group to look into this entire area. It started by looking at the full range of tasks which teachers are asked or expected to undertake, in order to see how teachers' administrative burden could be reduced.

The DfEE identified an extensive range of tasks, ranging from individual-centred tasks like lesson planning to institution-based tasks like recruitment.

Importantly, the Working Group also sought to identify the range and amount of data that schools and colleges are asked to supply to various organisations. This research has had important consequences, as it has led to the DfEE to consider what it has called the Common Basic Data Set, described below.

Approaching the problem of the administrative burden on teachers from the standpoint of the data rather than the tasks is potentially quite fruitful. A task-based perspective is useful for helping to identify those tasks which are not necessary, those which could be carried out by administrative staff or learning assistants, say, and those which could be carried out more efficiently by using computers. In other words, the task-based approach can help us to answer the questions posed earlier. However, the data-based approach leads to a number of questions about the amount of (superfluous) work involved in each task:

- Has this data already been entered into a computer system?
- Is the data I am being asked to supply similar to other data I have been asked to supply?
- Can this data be entered in a way which will enable it to be manipulated and reported upon in numerous ways?

What emerges from these sorts of questions are the following principles:

- Data should need to be entered once only; once entered, it can be used in several ways.
- Organisations requesting data from schools and colleges should ask for data in the same format – or, to put it another way, schools and colleges should not be obliged to provide data which is not in the commonly agreed format, or which has not been collected as part of the agreed data set.
- Data should be transferable electronically as far as possible, including electronic data interchange (EDI), optical mark reader (OMR), email, the internet and so on.

Returning to the first item in the list, namely that data should need to be entered only once, this idea is based on the principle known as 'Right First Time'. Many teachers find themselves having to write out lists of pupils for their markbooks, or for other purposes such as educational visits.

This kind of duplication is not necessary, and if you are asked to write out data that already exists on the computer system then, something is wrong. There is either a technical problem, such as poorly-designed software, inadequate training of office staff, or poor management.

The DfEE commissioned Coopers and Lybrand to undertake research for the Working Group. (See the Appendix for details.)

Practical outcomes

In practical terms, the DfEE has acted on the Report by:

- issuing a circular to teachers and head teachers giving advice on how to reduce the bureaucratic burden on teachers – also available from the internet;

- issuing a framework to Chief Education Officers and equivalents in England, outlining how LEAs can help reduce teachers' administrative burden;

- starting a systematic review of its own policies;

- considering the standardisation of a common basic data set (see below);

- investigating the scope for schools to buy goods and services over the internet;

- hosting discussions on what an administratively efficient school might look like in the near future; the results of which have been published on the internet (see Appendix);

- setting up a pilot to look at how schools can receive more information electronically (some preliminary results of which should be available at the Virtual Teachers' web site by the time you read this);

- devising a timetable of milestones to be achieved, including a request for the QCA to take the administrative burden into account when reviewing the National Curriculum;

- following on from the previous point, asking other Government agencies, such as OFSTED, to explicitly address this issue when dealing with schools and colleges.

The Common Basic Data Set

This will standardise the way in which organisations ask for a core set of data from schools and colleges. Companies which specialise in school and college administration software have been issued with a specification for the core data, and will be required to design their systems to support it. The use of the Common Basic Data Set to store and make data returns is planned to be piloted in 1999.

Schools and colleges could refuse to provide data which lies outside the parameters of the Common Basic Data Set. Alternatively, they would have the option of selling the information on a commercial basis.

The school of the future

The school of the future, by which we mean the next four or five years, will have administrative systems which support rather than detract from the teacher's role in raising pupil achievement.

In addition to the discussions mentioned above, the DfEE has established a project to demonstrate how schools of different types and sizes can set up efficient administrative systems. The project involves schools in Kent and Derby City LEAs. The DfEE intends to publish the results of the pilot study on the internet.

The project is being managed by Price Waterhouse and Coopers, who will be considering the following kinds of questions:

- Which activities can be reduced or taken away from teachers altogether?
- How could LEAs help to minimise the administrative burden on schools?
- What techniques and procedures can be developed which could be adapted for use by all schools in the UK?

■ How can small schools, which do not have the opportunity to benefit from economies of scale through the implementation of new systems and procedures, benefit from using ICT? This is an area where the National Grid for Learning could play an important role, especially in the provision of low-cost tools (see the Appendix for details).

Chapter 11

Promoting ICT

Introduction

Words like 'promotion' and 'marketing' conjure up images of trying to sell something to someone, which is precisely what you need to do.

There are several reasons that you need to devote some time and energy to raising or maintaining the profile of ICT, including the following:

- Teachers have to use IT in their (National Curriculum) subjects. By raising the profile of ICT you can help to make the prospect less daunting for those of them who are worried about the prospect.

- Research has indicated that pupils can benefit from using computers in all subjects, including non-National Curriculum ones. By bringing the possibility of ICT to the attention of their teachers, you potentially will be helping them.

- ICT is conspicuously expensive. By engaging in some marketing effort, you will be helping other staff, parents and Governors to see the benefits of the spending.

- By promoting ICT, you will also be helping to promote the school or college in which you work.

Suggestions for promoting ICT

Most of the suggestions made here are no different from what many teachers will be doing anyway. Some have already been mentioned elsewhere in this book.

The suggestions, each of which is expanded upon, are:

- make it useful;
- make it welcoming and accessible;
- be helpful;
- lead by example;
- get results;
- keep good displays;
- keep staff informed;
- keep Governors informed;
- keep parents informed.

Make it useful

People are more likely to take notice of anything you want to tell them if they think it will be useful for them. This is a matter of both content and delivery.

Announcing in a staff meeting that new fibre optic cabling has just been installed will be meaningless, and therefore of little interest, to most people. Announcing instead that steps have been taken to install or extend the computer network may be more interesting (although it's better to announce such things after the event in case something prevents it coming to fruition).

Even here, however, many people won't know what a network is, or of what practical use it might be for them. Perhaps it would be better to announce in a staff meeting that a new network has been installed, and that information about what it can do has been put on the staff notice board. Better still, give them an example of what they can do now that they could not (easily) do before.

The kind of things other staff tend to find useful are things that will make their lives easier, or that will help them help their pupils get better results. This especially applies to staff who are concerned about the amount of money being spent on ICT.

Pupils will find ICT useful when they can see that they can achieve an objective faster or better with ICT than without it. For some pupils an objective may be simply to produce a perfect piece of work. This is something that ICT helps to make possible. See 'Get results' below also.

Make it welcoming and accessible

There is an unfortunate tendency, particularly in secondary schools and colleges, to allow the ICT manager's office to look like the garden shed of a mad inventor. Bits of cables, half wired plugs, ancient monitors lying around – all of this tends to give the impression that you are entering into an arcane and mysterious world. This can have a very negative effect on people's willingness to try using ICT.

On a more day-to-day level, software and hardware should be welcoming in the sense of being easy to use. This means not only setting up the hardware and software to be easy to use, but also getting rid of any error messages that creep in after installing new software, because when an error message appears, users often think it is because of something that they have done. Responding to and sorting out problems rapidly – and being seen to do so – are extremely important.

If possible, set aside resources that are only for staff use. This could be computers in the staffroom, or a staff resources room, or it could be that staff are given priority over some equipment at certain times of the day. If equipment is set aside solely for staff use, such as in a staffroom, it should be the best equipment available. Having equipment that staff may borrow is also a very good idea.

Where groups of staff want to discuss the use of ICT in their subject areas or their classrooms, invite them to use the computer room (if there is one) for their meeting, or offer to be on hand. This will enable them to answer some questions straight away, such as 'Do we have program X?', or 'Do the pupils know how to use program X?' or 'How many computers are there in the computer room?'.

Pupils also need to find ICT welcoming. Again, computer error messages which are unrelated to anything the user is doing should be eradicated. Equipment should be kept clean and in good condition generally: it is horrible to have to use a keyboard whose keys are filthy, for example. As a general rule, if you or other staff wouldn't want to use something, why expect the pupils to do so?

ICT can also be made welcoming to pupils in the form of extra-curricular activities such as lunchtime clubs, homework clubs and so on. If pupils have to book to use the facilities, this should be easy to do. Computers should have manuals and posters near them showing how to start and finish, and possibly how to use the basic features of the main programs available.

Also, pay attention to comfort, especially in the area of air conditioning.

Manuals, posters and tidiness are also essential in making the computer resources more welcoming and accessible.

Be helpful

Helping other staff to achieve something they could not do before helps to induce a positive attitude towards you and, therefore, ICT. It also helps to avoid the situation where people think ICT is 'rubbish' because they cannot do what they want to do.

It is important to understand that word of mouth has long been recognised as often more important than advertising in the business world. Also, it costs much more to gain a new customer than it does to retain an existing one. Translated into the educational environment, this means that how we respond to requests for assistance can not only affect how each individual will feel towards using ICT in the future, but may also have an influence on other people's attitude through the word of mouth route.

Although you may have to say 'no' to some requests, either because of the nature of the task or because of time constraints, you should follow it up by giving some assistance. Reluctant users will not feel inclined to try ICT, or to co-operate with you, if they experience your attitude as being unhelpful or obstructive.

The kind of help you may be able to offer even when you are unable to help includes:

- running an ICT surgery at a designated time;
- offering to help at a more convenient time, such as after school;
- offering to lend or give the person a guide or a manual;
- offering to show them how to do it for themselves at a mutually convenient time;
- telling them who else, including pupils , may be able to help them.

One of the things that pupils find frustrating is not being able to get help from the teacher at the time they need it. It is therefore a good idea to provide alternative means of assistance, and to make sure that users know what these are. Alternative types of assistance can include:

- help cards next to the computer(s);
- guides next to the computer(s);
- posters on the walls;
- classroom assistants if available;
- using the in-built Help present in most program.

Lead by example

In one school I worked in, someone had *written* a word processing manual. This was a useful manual, but because it had not been word processed, it had no effect on promoting the use of the word processor.

Leading by example means using ICT to:

- produce guides about using ICT;
- produce class registers;
- label cupboards, books, diskettes, an so on;
- create display headings on walls (see below).

Depending on your particular circumstances, it may also mean being seen to take advantage of the internet and email, and maintaining the school's or college's web site, or part of it. (If pupils can take charge of most of the work involved, and the decisions involved, in maintaining a web site, this is all to the good.)

Get results

The best way of promoting ICT amongst pupils is to make sure they get results. If as a result of using ICT they produce better work – not only in ICT but in other areas of the curriculum too – they will want to carry on using it.

This means, amongst other things, putting in place a scheme of work that facilitates progression as pupils move up through the year groups, and which incorporates differentiation. It could also entail awarding certificates to pupils as they achieve certain levels of expertise. In some cases, especially at secondary level, pupils can be entered for certified courses at the end of modules of work or at the end of each academic year.

Keep good displays

The rules governing ICT displays are the same as for any other subject. They should be:

- produced on computer to at least some extent;
- interesting;
- tidy;
- kept up to date;
- useful;
- free of spelling errors;
- a showcase for pupils' work.

You are not restricted to paper or wall displays either. If you have the room, you can make an interesting display of computer history, or of parts of a computer. Encourage other teachers to put up ICT-related displays also.

Keep staff informed

This is related to the first point, about making ICT useful for people, in the sense that people will only find something useful if they know about it.

You can keep staff informed through:

- occasional announcements in staff meetings;
- occasional bulletins in the staff briefing sheet, if there is one;
- regular bulletins about the work covered in IT lessons, if applicable, so that staff know what they can expect pupils in different year groups to be able to do in IT;
- notices on the staff noticeboard – preferably in a specific space dedicated to ICT-related notices;
- an ICT newsletter containing useful information.

You may be asked to provide senior management with information every so often, but you can offer to do so anyway. The kinds of things that senior staff are interested in knowing about include:

- statistics on the extent to which computers are being used, both in the curriculum and outside it;
- changes in procedures, new equipment and software, new courses;
- information relating to the effects of the ICT provision on pupils' behaviour and achievement, and success stories.

Keep Governors informed

You may be asked to contribute to the Head's report to the Governing Body every so often. If this is voluntary, volunteer, because by keeping a high profile you may be able to secure extra funding in the future. Another reason for keeping Governors informed is that some of them may be able to provide the school with useful equipment that is being disposed of by companies.

If you are asked to write a report on ICT, whether for Governors or senior staff, provide a summary of the main points at the start of the report, and keep technical details to a minimum (unless specifically asked to provide them).

Keep parents informed

Many parents are interested in computers and how they are being used in their child's education. It is a good idea to keep parents informed about what is going on. Bear in mind also that some parents become Governors, and that parents talk to each other about what is going on in the school.

Ways in which you can keep parents informed about ICT include:

- contributing to any newsletters which the Headteacher sends to parents;
- being involved in open evenings/days;
- making sure that there are rolling presentations on a computer in a prominent place, such as the school entrance;
- staging special events for parents, such as an evening devoted to explaining how ICT is being used throughout the curriculum, or about the new course being introduced in Year 8, or an exhibition of how pupils in Year 4 used ICT on a recent school trip;
- organising an open day or evening when parents can try out the programs for themselves – with the assistance of pupil helpers – and can look at the sort of work that goes on;
- arranging for parents to help out with lessons, subject to the usual precautions.

Chapter 12
Managing INSET

Planning INSET

What planning the INSET involves

Planning IT INSET involves four main stages:

1 Understand the possible reasons for delivering IT INSET.

2 Prioritise the INSET requirements in your institution.

3 Decide on the most appropriate form of delivery.

4 Organise the INSET.

Each of these involves sub-stages.

Reasons for IT INSET

It is important to identify the reasons for delivering IT INSET because the purpose of training affects other factors, such as how it is delivered, where it is delivered, who delivers it, who should attend and how long it takes.

The main reasons for running IT INSET are to enable staff to:

■ understand the capabilities of ICT;

■ identify opportunities in their schemes of work for using ICT;

- learn how to use the hardware effectively;
- learn how to use the software effectively;
- trouble-shoot effectively;
- use computers in their lessons;
- assess pupils' computer-based work;
- use computers for their own administration;
- keep informed about official requirements;
- further develop their skills portfolio.

Let's look into each of these a little further, in order to identify what is required in each case.

INSET on the capabilities of ICT

Before staff will be able to identify meaningful opportunities in their schemes of work for using ICT they will need to know what kind of things you can do with computers. They will already have a general idea from listening to the news and reading newspapers and magazines. However, what is important here is that they understand how it can be used in, for example:

- their own subject area;
- the National Literacy Project;
- the National Numeracy Strategy.

Closely allied to this is knowledge about how to use computers for administrative purposes, such as recording marks (see page 145).

Identify appropriate opportunities for using ICT

The National Curriculum Programmes of Study make it quite clear that pupils are to be given opportunities to apply their IT skills to the subject 'where appropriate'. Even if or when the wording of the Programmes of Study changes to make this requirement much more specific, many teachers will still need assistance in identifying opportunities.

Quite often, teachers wish to use computers in their lessons, but do not know enough about them and what they can do. This leads to an understandable lack of confidence. However, once teachers have been introduced to and have understood the type of things that computers can be used for in a particular area of the curriculum, they will naturally start to identify opportunities themselves if they genuinely want to.

INSET in this area is most effective when it focuses on processes rather than skills. The aim is to see how far the processes involved in the subject can be accommodated, made easier, or made more interesting through the use of ICT.

Here is a list of some of the approaches you might like to consider:

- In subjects that involve calculation, computers can remove extraneous factors. For example, using a pre-prepared spreadsheet to explore number patterns means that pupils can experiment with large numbers without risking the errors which could arise from using a calculator, such as pressing the wrong key.

- If calculators are not available, spreadsheets make it possible to use numbers that would be too large to be worked with otherwise.

- In subjects where evidence has to be looked at and evaluated, the use of a database to keep track of findings can be extremely useful.

- Computers can be used to depict situations that would otherwise be difficult or impossible to depict in a classroom. For example, pupils could use a database to identify wildlife, or could use a modelling program to test the effects of wind on a car travelling at speed.

- Computers make it possible to change your mind over and over again, and still produce a perfect-looking result, on time.

In all of these cases (and this list is by no means exhaustive), we are, in effect, asking the following questions:

> 1 What do you actually *do* in the subject you are teaching? For example, do you search through documents, manipulate numbers, process text...?

2 What can computers be made to do?

  3 Are there ways in which the answers to questions 1 and
     2 can be combined to reveal how computers can be
     made to do (or to enhance or illustrate) what you do in
     your subject?

Use the hardware effectively

In order to start to use the computers, whether for their
administration or in lessons, staff need to know how to:

- log on to the system, or start up the computers;
- log off from the system, or shut down the computers;
- use the printer;
- put paper in the printer;
- use the demonstration system if you have one, including items
  like a large monitor or an interactive whiteboard;
- use other peripherals where relevant, such as scanners.

In principle, these are the kinds of things that staff may prefer to hear
about on a need-to-know basis. However, the trouble with this sort of
ad hoc approach is that you could, in theory, end up repeating exactly
the same information several times a week. Therefore, a more
structured approach is required in addition to the casual approach.

Use the software effectively

Staff also need to know how to use the software as well as the
hardware. There are several levels and kinds of software expertise,
including knowledge and understanding of:

- how to perform basic tasks like opening, closing, saving and
  printing documents;
- how to carry out more advanced processes, such as automating
  procedures through macros, for example, or by customising the
  interface of programs (some allow you to change the appearance
  of the menus and icons, for instance);
- how to use features of the software in furtherance of their own
  teaching objectives;
- how to use highly subject-specific software.

Trouble-shoot effectively

Most people who use the computer facilities will not know how it works, or how to fix it when it breaks down – including even you perhaps. However, it certainly makes everybody's life much easier if they can hazard an educated guess at why things appear to be going wrong. It will also help to give them the confidence they need to use computers in their lessons.

Things to cover in a trouble-shooting course include:

- knowing the correct names for different parts of the computer system;
- how to do trouble-shooting by going through a logical checklist (starting with: is it plugged in?);
- why certain things may happen; for example, printing on a network will slow down appreciably if everyone tries to print large graphics at the same time;
- what to do in the event of a disaster, including ways of helping to ensure that work is not lost – or at least not too much of it;
- things that will help to avoid the disaster happening in the first place.

Use computers in their lessons

Using computers in lessons is very different from either not using them, or using them for one's own work, or allowing pupils to use them in a fairly unstructured way. Using computers in lessons requires teachers to have a range of skills, such as an ability to:

- identify useful applications for computers in the curriculum;
- draw up a rota of access if there are too few computers in the classroom for everyone to use them at the same time;
- make very rapid judgements as to whether real work is going on, both at the computer and at the tables or desks;
- not get flustered when a pupil asks them a question about the software that they cannot answer.

Although a lot of this comes with practice, the kinds of skills involved are really no different from teaching skills in general.

Assess pupils' computer-based work

It is sometimes difficult for teachers to distinguish between process and outcome, leading them to evaluate the quality of the pupil's learning by the quality of the output s/he has produced.

These days, it is easy to produce a professional-looking document in minutes — even seconds if all you have to do is hit the print button from within an encyclopaedia on a CD-ROM.

Even where this isn't the case, teachers have a tendency to become mesmerised by the apparently arcane knowledge possessed by a large number of young people.

Teachers need to be taught to understand the following:

- Many pupils who use computers a lot, especially those who have a computer at home, are often working at a very unsophisticated level in terms of the software's capabilities.

- The criteria for evaluating IT skills should be based on the thinking processes required. For example, an **appropriate** simple bar chart shows better understanding of the subject in hand than a sophisticated, but totally **inappropriate**, three dimensional exploded pie chart.

- Pupils have always produced work that looks good but which, on closer inspection, turns out to have been copied from a book wholesale, or irrelevant, or not really understood by the person handing it in. Spotting poor work produced on a computer is, ultimately, no more difficult than spotting poor work produced by any other means, but some teachers will need to be told this.

Use computers for their own administration

There is evidence from portable computer projects that staff who use computers for their own administration will begin to feel less reluctant to use them in lessons.

Even were this not the case, it would still be a good idea to teach staff how computers can lessen their workload. One of the problems faced by many ICT managers is that they work in an institution where the culture is almost tangibly anti-computer. Showing staff how computers can benefit them personally is one way of starting to break down the barriers, and change the culture of the institution.

The kinds of knowledge and skills which many teachers require include:

- how to access pupil data from the administrative network;
- how to produce lists of pupils, perhaps in a different order than their class registers;
- how to save time by creating and using templates in word processing and other programs;
- how to keep track of pupil grades, spending, merit certificates awarded for good behaviour, and so on.

See Chapter 10 for more ideas.

Keep informed about official requirements

Forewarned is forearmed. If staff know, or have a good inkling, that what is required of them is about to change, they can better prepare for it.

If, by using ICT, they can keep themselves up to date on matters that affect them, that will be all the better.

The kind of knowledge to pass on includes:

- announcements by bodies like the DfEE and the QCA;
- new national reports by OFSTED;
- new Green Papers and White Papers.
- information and publications produced by other organisations, such as BECTa;
- how to access reports and keep up to date by using the internet;
- how to access new, or newly-discovered, web sites.

Further develop their skills portfolio

Many schools and colleges these days are looking for some degree of IT competence in new staff. Some of your colleagues may appreciate INSET that will enhance their marketability in the long run.

This highlights the problem of any training: that once trained, good staff may move on. This will be a risk whatever INSET you run. If you organise INSET that leads to external qualifications, you have to ensure that the training benefits the institution in which you work. Therefore, to give a simple example, if you work in a primary school it would be better to organise basic word processing courses than courses in programming (except for variants of LOGO perhaps).

The kinds of courses available include:

- certificates in single application skills, such as word processing, desktop publishing and so on;
- certificates in combined application skills, such as certificates in general IT skills, or databases and spreadsheets combined;
- certificates in the use of IT in an educational setting.

Prioritising INSET

In order to effectively prioritise IT INSET, you have to have the following information:

1. A knowledge of where the school is going – this is one reason you need to have an ICT Strategy in place (see Chapter 2).

2. A knowledge of where the school is – which usually means carrying out an audit of staff IT skills (see below).

3. A plan for getting from (1) to (2).

The staff IT skills audit

There are several kinds of audit you can use, ranging from the very brief to the very in-depth approach. Seeing as no audit is going to be entirely accurate unless you give staff what amounts to a practical test, the brief version might prove to be the better option. It has the distinct advantage that, being relatively short, you will probably get most returned within the deadline you set, with few people moaning about the extra work involved.

It is useful to include a question or two about the teacher's competence and confidence in using computers in lessons. An example of a staff skills audit is given in Figure 12.1. (You may prefer to go through this sheet with individual members of staff rather than simply plonk it in their pigeon holes.)

Staff IT Skills Audit

Name _____ (Department, if applicable _____)

Applications

Please circle the description that most accurately describes your skills in each of the following areas. Please do not be unduly modest!

Word processing*	Very good	Good	Fair	Poor	Very poor
Databases	Very good	Good	Fair	Poor	Very poor
Spreadsheets	Very good	Good	Fair	Poor	Very poor
Desktop publishing	Very good	Good	Fair	Poor	Very poor
Control/programming	Very good	Good	Fair	Poor	Very poor
Data-logging	Very good	Good	Fair	Poor	Very poor
Other (please specify)	Very good	Good	Fair	Poor	Very poor

*You may prefer to substitute actual program names.

What do you feel is your general level of competence in using ICT?	Very good	Good	Fair	Poor	Very poor

If you have any qualifications in IT, please list them here, and the approximate dates you gained them:

Do you use computers in your lessons?	Very often	Often	Sometimes	Rarely
How confident are you in using computers in lessons?	Very		Fairly	Not very
How easy do you find computers in lessons?	Very		Fairly	Not very
Any other comments/ your requests?				

Figure 12.1 – Staff IT skills audit

Once the skills audits have been completed and returned, you need to analyse them. A useful tool here is a spreadsheet, because this will enable you to see what percentage of staff consider themselves to be very good, good and so on in each area.

Many spreadsheet packages have a built-in function that will enable you to carry out that sort of analysis. However, a quick way of achieving the same result is to use or assign numerical values to the descriptions. For example, very good could be 5, good 4 and so on.

The results of the audit cannot in themselves dictate what INSET is required. For example, only 10% of teachers may consider themselves to be good at using control programs – and that may be twice as many as the school needs. You will have to make a judgement about which areas to target, and therefore which staff to target.

You may decide to target those staff who feel competent in using ICT, but who lack confidence in using computers in lessons. You may even find the reverse in some cases: staff who consider themselves to be confident and competent in using ICT in lessons, but do not consider themselves to be particularly good at using computers. You may find it profitable to use the audit questionnaire as a starting point in each of these cases, following up with a brief chat with the member of staff concerned.

You may wish to amend the questionnaire shown in Figure 12.1 to include a question about staff use of computers for their administrative work.

The audit is useful not only for the purpose of planning INSET, but also, in a secondary school or college, for helping you decide who you would like to be involved in the teaching of IT, if this is applicable and if you have some say in the matter.

The exercise will need to be repeated at least once a year, or more often if there is a high degree of staff turnover.

Organising the IT INSET

Your INSET plan should:

- work on a similar time scale to your ICT Strategy, because it is one of the factors that will help to bring the ICT Strategy to fruition;
- take into account the requirements of the ICT Strategy;
- take into consideration the strengths and weaknesses of the staff, as indicated by the audit (see above).

The kind of INSET you plan should fit into the institution's overall development plan and INSET plan. Therefore, once you have drawn up your own scheme be sure to discuss it with the appropriate person – especially as it will usually have financial implications of one kind or another.

Each of your proposed INSET sessions should also be appropriate to its objectives. The following section highlights the types of INSET model available.

Types of INSET

Just as there is no one type of lesson that is suitable for all pupils and any subject, so there is no one type of INSET that is appropriate in all circumstances. The following list summarises the main approaches to choose from.

Whole staff INSET

This is appropriate for disseminating information, whether about ICT in your establishment or new Government rules. However, it is not always appropriate for giving practical instruction unless it is planned very carefully, and as part of a long term strategy.

Many senior teachers make the mistake of thinking that one school INSET day is sufficient, and the appropriate delivery mode, for significantly and more or less permanently raising teachers' ICT skills. It is usually better to have a narrower focus than an all-embracing one, and build in time for discussing how the skills acquired, or the software seen, could be used in the curriculum.

You might consider dispensing with practical sessions altogether: why not show a video, possibly produced in-house, illustrating the kinds of things that can be done with computers? Perhaps computers could be set up for staff to use throughout the day on a drop-in basis?

Small group training

Practical training is best done with specific groups. These groups could be based on:

- ability, such as all those who described themselves as generally not very good at using ICT;
- subject, such as Literacy, or departmental groupings in secondary schools and colleges;
- software, such as basic word processing;
- type of staff, such as new staff, trainee teachers, senior management.

An example of small group training is an induction course run for staff who have just joined. The induction course will include practical information about how to log on to the computers, where the printing will come out, and so on. Of course, in small schools the entire staff may constitute a small group.

Individual training

This is very costly in terms of your time, and so the potential benefits and costs need to be weighed carefully.

However, you can supply independent learning materials in a cost-effective way, either through manuals, posters and instruction sheets, or by learning modules made available on an intranet. This approach can be very cost-effective because by and large there is only a one-off cost involved – although you will need to update the materials every so often.

Principles of IT INSET

Any IT INSET you provide should:

- relate any software skills covered to the curriculum, and to using the program in the classroom;
- help to build staff confidence;
- help staff to become independent learners.

Who does the training?

You do not have to provide all of the training yourself. In fact, you do not even have to do the audit yourself, or draw up the INSET plan yourself. These activities can often be carried out by an ICT Committee, preferably under your leadership.

- The skills audit may indicate other staff who could run some courses.
- It is also possible to cascade the training, meaning that you train some people, who in turn train others.
- Your LEA advisory service may run relevant courses.
- It may be possible to collaborate with other schools in the area.
- School staff may be able to attend INSET or other courses at a local college.
- For certain kinds of training, such as New Opportunities Fund (NOF) training, you will have to choose from a list of accredited training providers. (These can be either local or national.)
- Hardware and software suppliers sometimes include a day's training in the price of the package.
- There are training companies and independent consultants. These are sometimes cost-effective solutions to training, but it is important to use a company or an individual consultant who has experience in education.
- There may be training available via email or a web site.

Accredited courses

Offering staff the possibility of (external) accreditation is a good way of providing them with an incentive to learn, and a reward for attending. Staff often see external accreditation as important for future job prospects.

There are relatively few courses which focus on the educational use of ICT, as opposed to merely software skills. Nevertheless, software skills courses can be useful, not just for the obvious reasons but also because having a certificate or two does tend to raise self-confidence.

For details of possible courses, contact the Examination Boards listed in the Appendix (but note that other organisations not listed run courses too).

The overall INSET plan

Your completed INSET plan will probably consist of a mixture of approaches. Perhaps there will be a range of self-supported study materials for all staff to use. Perhaps you will recommend that one or two staff go on courses run by your LEA advisory team, while others may attend a one-off session at a local college.

The point here is that your job is to draw up the plan, but it should not follow that you also have to do all of the training as well – although unfortunately that is often the case.

INSET costs

These days, everything has to take account of cost, and INSET is no exception to the rule. Costs fall into three main categories, these being:

- explicit costs, such as the cost of enrolling on a course, buying materials like videos, or hiring a speaker;
- semi-hidden costs, such as cover provision for teachers on courses;
- hidden costs in the form of opportunity costs, ie what you and others could have been doing instead of preparing for or attending a course.

When drawing up your INSET plan, you should consider the following questions. Even if you cannot answer them completely accurately, the process of trying to is an important one to go through.

- What are the true costs of the proposed courses?
- What are the likely benefits, in terms of the fulfilment of the ICT Strategy?

■ Do the expected benefits exceed the costs?

■ Have the right staff to attend the courses been identified? It is not cost-effective to incur the costs of training supply teachers, for example, unless they are in the school for a term or longer, or there is little or no extra cost involved, such as on a whole staff INSET day. If there is a choice between training a teacher or training the person fulfilling a role, the latter should take precedent, even if that means deferring the training. For example, If the teacher of class 2a is on maternity leave, her place on a training course should not be taken by an agency teacher, unless that could be justified in some way.

■ Have the most appropriate courses been identified?

■ Have the most appropriate modes of delivery been identified?

■ Is the INSET plan still relevant in the light of recent staff changes, changes in curricular requirements etc?

An INSET plan which takes into account the factors listed in this chapter is more likely to be successful in meeting the needs of the ICT Strategy than one which is either unplanned or which is merely a response to the requests of others.

Chapter 13
The internet

Introduction

The Government has set a target of every school, library, college and university being connected to the internet by 2002 (see 'Our Information Age', on the Number-10 web site, listed in the Appendix). Senior management teams need to consider rules governing teachers' and pupils' access to the internet. This should be approached as part of a well-thought out policy, not in an ad hoc fashion.

The potential benefits and costs of the internet

The potential benefits of the internet

The internet and its related technologies – intranets, extranets, email, the world wide web and Usenet newsgroups, together with Internet Relay Chat and similar communications systems – is arguably one of the most important inventions this century, or ever. (In the business world, an extranet is, in effect, an intranet to which access has been extended to customers and suppliers. Applied to a school or college, it would include, for example, parents, other schools, the LEA and others.) Unfortunately, it has been dogged by a lot of hype that does not reflect the current reality of most people's experience.

What the internet means from a management perspective is speed, and potentially lower costs. The speed factor comes into play both in terms of acquiring information and purchasing products. Moreover, using the internet can often cut out many costs.

We in the UK have been slower than others, especially North Americans, in taking up the use of the internet, but its use in all walks of life is increasing. It has vast potential in schools and colleges in terms of management. Some possibilities which suggest themselves are:

- sharing good practice with colleagues from other institutions or even other countries;
- working collaboratively with colleagues across distances;
- gaining access to official reports as soon as they have been published;
- undertaking 'armchair' research into different products;
- purchasing products through the internet equivalent of mail order;
- exchanging data between educational institutions;
- exchanging data between schools and official agencies such as the QCA;
- exchanging data between schools and other organisations, such as Examining Boards;
- providing access to lesson plans and other curriculum material, and policy documents;
- providing access to a vast range of resources by staff and pupils alike;
- providing information, including the prospectus, to parents and others in the community;
- providing a forum for Governors to discuss ideas and issues;
- providing a means of pupils (or their parents) sending in and collecting work from home;
- promoting the school or college by means of having a web site.

The potential benefits of an intranet

Potential benefits of an intranet – even without access to the internet – include:

- (in the case of a secondary school or college) sharing good practice with colleagues from other departments or buildings;
- having instant access to official reports held by the school, such as the report of its last OFSTED inspection, or QCA guidelines on the Key Stages 1 and 2 curriculum;
- having instant access to the school or college prospectus and policy documents;
- having instant access to the school or college pro formas, such as letters to parents about school trips or school uniform, INSET application forms and so on;
- having access to lesson plans and other curriculum material, and policy documents;
- having access to a vast range of resources by staff and pupils alike (including resources downloaded from the internet and checked, and then saved on the local system);
- providing information, including the prospectus, to parents and others in the community;
- providing a forum for Governors to discuss ideas and issues;
- providing a means of gathering information, through the use of on-line forms, such as for budget estimates, requests for money, IT skills audit and so on;
- extending the useful life of older equipment (see below);
- providing a means of pupils handing in and collecting work.

One of the problems experienced by just about every school or college in the country is that of uneven development of computer systems and software. Thus it is not uncommon to find, say, that three different versions of Word are in use: Word 2, Word 6 and Word 97.

This is a situation that is discussed in Chapter 9. It is suggested there that one way to at least partially overcome the problems associated with different versions of the same software package is to encourage people to use utilities like the Word 6 viewer supplied free by Microsoft, in order to read, though not alter, Word 6 documents. There are not viewers for all programs, and the viewers do not let you do anything except view and print, but this approach is better than nothing.

An even better solution is to establish a school or college intranet, because of all the advantages of transferability and transparency. This means that, with a few relatively minor exceptions, if you have the right software, ie a web browser, you can view any document on the intranet, without having to be concerned about what program was used to create it, or what kind of computer it is stored on.

Thus a school or college based intranet can be useful for extending the effective life of older equipment and software.

There are also some exciting new developments involving the linking up of several schools and other institutions, as in the Bristol Education Online Network – see the Appendix for more information. Recently, the Bristol Education Intranet was launched. This links Bristol's 117 schools to the LEA's education offices, the internet and SuperJanet, an education network.

The potential costs of the internet

Unfortunately, there is no such thing as a free lunch, and the internet is no exception. Some of the management costs associated with the internet and related technologies are:

- managing the use of a single computer connected to the internet;
- deciding on the most appropriate technology to use to connect the school or college to the internet (a single computer connection is very limited in what it allows you to achieve);
- ensuring that value-added services which provide access to curriculum materials on subscription are used in a way and to an extent that justifies the cost;
- controlling the volume of email traffic within the organisation;
- keeping control of telephone charges where applicable;
- controlling emailing from staff and pupils to other people both within and outside the organisation.
- preventing pupils gaining access to undesirable materials, such as through an internet service provider's subscription charges for a filtered service;
- preventing pupils wasting time, and perhaps even putting themselves at risk, through on-line chat and email.

These issues are covered in the next section.

Internet-related management issues

Using a single computer connected to the internet

Where you have a single computer connected to the internet, you will need to address the following points.

- Where will it be located? It is more accurate to say that there is a single user internet account rather than a single computer connected to the internet. In principle, there is no reason why several stand-alone computers cannot be set up to be able to connect to the internet, as long as no more than one user tries to do so at the same time – which is in itself hard to manage centrally. The ideal location is probably the one which will allow the greatest degree of supervised access.

- Who will be able to use it? Will it be used only in the context of lessons, or outside lessons too? If the latter, on what basis will some pupils be allowed to use it? This could be according to Year group (for example, Year 4 on Monday), a first come first served basis, a booking system, or according to what the would-be user wants to use it for.

- When will staff be able to access it?

- How will its use be incorporated into lesson plans and schemes of work?

- How will staff and pupils be taught how to make the best use of the internet? This involves more than just the technical aspects of how to get on-line – the computer should be set up to make this process as easy as clicking on an icon. There are also the more important matters of how to use search engines properly, how to evaluate web sites and materials and how to download or save materials discovered. There are also wider issues like copyright matters that everybody who uses the internet should be encouraged to consider.

Deciding on the most appropriate technology

A dial-up connection is very slow compared with other solutions.

Considerations to be addressed include:

- Is technology X likely to be an expensive dead-end? (It might be better to wait until an industry standard emerges, say.)
- How should the school/college network (if there is one) be set up in order to be able to access both the internet and an intranet?
- Where can I turn for independent technical advice? The first port of call for most schools will be their LEA.

Subscription services

Many companies are starting to provide access to curriculum materials and administrative tools. Sometimes, these services also provide a solution to telephone charges. The problem with the usual call charging system, apart from the cost itself, is the fact the bill is unknown in advance, and so cannot be planned for accurately. An all-in-one subscription service can solve this problem.

For a subscription to a service that provides web content to be cost-effective, the following conditions should apply:

- The content should be of a high quality: if people would not use it (or adapt it for use) in their classroom, there is no point in having it.
- Ideally, the content should be UK-based, or at least relevant to the National Curriculum.
- The content should be appropriate to the users in question, eg Year 4.
- To an increasing extent, the web content should be exclusive to that provider. It is fairly easy to find good quality material on the web, despite the fact that there is lots of it, and growing all the time. For a subscription service to be worthwhile, it should have content that you cannot find elsewhere.
- There should be value-added features. For example, research tools for pupils to use, administrative tools for teachers to use, and areas in which people can exchange ideas.
- There should be links to educational bodies and periodicals, both exclusively on-line publications and internet versions of paper publications.

- Content should be filtered, or the browser software provided should include a filtering option. This could save you the cost of buying or subscribing to filter software separately (see below).

Controlling email traffic

There needs to be a clear policy on email usage, both for staff and pupils. There are several issues to be considered:

- Is it necessary to deliver the message by email? Answering emails takes time, but what people do not always appreciate is that checking to see how an email needs to be responded to also takes time. It may only take 30 seconds to read through the message and take a decision, but if there are 30 messages to be considered that amounts to 15 minutes. One point to be included in any policy should perhaps be that only work-related messages should be sent. Jokes downloaded from the internet are all very well, but they can waste time – and physically clog up the system and make it work slower as well.

- Communication by email with outsiders should be treated in the same way as letters, phone calls and faxes. If it is the institution's policy that senior staff must read and approve letters and faxes before they are sent, the same rule should apply to email messages.

- If there is no such rule, staff should be made aware of the fact that any derogatory remarks made about anyone in an email message is just as subject to the laws of libel as would be the case if they'd put the remarks in a letter. As a general rule, if you wouldn't put something in a memo, fax or letter, don't put it in an email.

- Pupils have to learn to use email sensibly too. It seems to be the case quite often that pupils waste time at first sending silly (and sometimes rude) messages to each other, and this has to be watched out for. Perhaps more serious is the situation where pupils are sending personal information, like their phone number, to people they do not know.

- What language issues are there? Email messages are a cross between the formality of a letter and the informality of a phone call. Should people err on the side of formality or informality, generally speaking? Also, three letter acronyms (TLAs) and 'smilies' are often used. Should they be?

Clearly, in many of these cases, what is required is training in the proper use of email, a set of guidelines to be available quickly by people when they are working at the computer, and a school policy on the matter (perhaps as a subset of an Acceptable Use Policy – see below).

Controlling telephone charges where applicable

How can telephone charges be minimised? Some suggestions:

- Encourage people to download (save) web pages, and look at them off-line. There are some utilities available that enable you to save web sites – but if you buy one, make sure it is set up to download only down to a few levels, and no external links, otherwise the web site capturing process itself can take a very long time.

- Read and respond to email messages off-line.

- Another option is to negotiate cheap or free phone charges in school hours. Where a lot of usage is expected, you should consider subscribing to a service which provides web content and a one-off call charge per annum (see below). Be aware that these deals do not always take into account the increasing demand for out-of-hours schooling, such as homework clubs or summer schools.

Preventing access to undesirable materials

Most people's idea of 'undesirable' materials is pornography. However, there are five main kinds of undesirable materials:

- materials which are not relevant to the learning objectives being addressed at the time;

- pornography;

- racist material and other examples of bigotry, including biased and/or inaccurate depiction of historical events;

- instructions on how to harm other people;

- encouragement to break the law in other ways, such as through drug growing.

It is important to make these distinctions, for two reasons:

- What is undesirable in some contexts may not be undesirable in others. For example, it may be important for pupils in a politics class to look at racist web sites as part of their studies.

- Because the problem is different in each case, there is not one foolproof solution that will satisfactorily address all of them.

There are five main ways of addressing the issue of undesirable materials, these being:

- the software solution;
- filtered service from an internet service provider;
- supervision;
- trust;
- an Acceptable Use Policy.

We will now consider these in more detail.

The software solution

This takes two main forms:

- Access to sites listed in the software's database is blocked, or access to a list of sites is granted; this kind of solution is only useful if you take out a subscription in order to keep getting the updated list of sites.
- Searches are scanned for certain keywords, and the operation stopped if they are found. This is a blunt instrument, which can prevent access to sites you do want pupils to look at (such as ones dealing with breast cancer) while not always preventing access to tasteless sites discovered by quite innocent searches.

Filtered service

This is where an internet service provider creates, or provides links to, educational web content. Undesirable sites are screened out as part of the service.

Supervision

Although it is impossible to closely monitor everyone's activities on the internet at the time, often the mere presence of a teacher in charge can help to prevent abuses. Staff should be aware of the fact that it is not always possible to see obscene or dangerous material from a distance.

It is a good idea to set up automatic monitoring software if possible. Then, if people try to access undesirable sites when nobody else is around, you may be able to track down who it was.

Trust

With older students, such as in 6th form or at college, it is sometimes possible to approach the problem with the attitude of 'I am trusting you to not try to access pornographic web sites (say); please do not abuse that trust.'.

Unfortunately, this does not provide reassurance for parents who expect their children to be vigorously protected from such material.

An Acceptable Use Policy

This sets out the expected code of conduct of pupils, and the consequences of breaking the rules. It should also state what the school or college will do to try to protect pupils, perhaps adding a disclaimer to the effect that it is impossible to guarantee 100% protection.

There are examples of Acceptable Use Policies on the world wide web. Most of these are American, but they can be adapted for use in this country (see the Appendix).

The solution

What is needed is a combination of all these approaches, because none of them in isolation offers a complete solution.

These four partial solutions need to be bound together by the school's internet policy. Just as there is a health and safety policy and many other types of policy, so there should be a school or college internet policy which addresses all of the areas covered in this chapter.

Appendix

This appendix carries a list of useful resources for the ICT manager. In addition to the general ones listed, there are also specific resources for most chapters.

General

Books and other publications

Croner's Guide to IT, Croner Publications.

DfEE: *Connecting the Learning Society*, 1997.

DfEE: *Excellence in Cities*, 1999.

DfEE: *Information Technology in the National Curriculum*, 1995.

DfEE: *Open for Learning, Open for Business*, 1998.

DfEE: *Survey of Information and Communications Technology in Schools 1998*, November 1998.

DfEE: *Teaching: High Status, High Standards – Requirements for Courses of Initial Teacher Training*, Circular Number 4/98, May 1998.

DfEE: *The National Curriculum*, 1995.

Harrison, Mike: *Coordinating information & communications technology across the Primary School*, Falmer Press, 1998.

Lock, Dennis (Ed): *The Gower Book of Management*, 1998.

NCET/NAACE: *Implementing IT*, 1997.

Poole, Phil (Ed): *Talking About Information and Communication Technology in Subject Teaching*, Canterbury Christ Church University College, 1998.

QCA: *Developing the School Curriculum*, 1998.

QCA: *Key Stage 4 Curriculum in Action*, 1998.

QCA/DfEE: *Information Technology: A scheme of work for Key Stages 1 and 2*, 1998.

SCAA: *Consistency in Teacher Assessment: Exemplification of Standards, Key Stage 3*, 1996.

SCAA: *Monitoring the School Curriculum: Reporting to Schools*, 1996.

Somekh, Bridget and Davis, Niki: *Using Information Technology Effectively in Teaching and Learning*, Routledge, 1997.

Stevenson, D: *Information and Communications Technology in UK Schools: An Independent Enquiry* (available from http://rubble.ultralab.anglia.ac.uk/stevenson/contents.html).

Williams, Gareth: *Information Technology Student Handbook*, Pearson Publishing, 1998.

Periodicals

Computer Education: The Computer Education Group, Computer Centre, Staffordshire University, School of Computing, Stafford ST18 0AD.

Computers Don't Bite: http://www.bbc.co.uk/education/cdb/

Educational Computing and Technology: http://www.ect.hobsons.com/ Tel: 01223 354 551

InTegrate: National Association for Co-ordinators and Teachers of IT (ACITT), Westbury Centre, Ripple Road, Barking, Essex IG11 7PT http://www.acitt.org.uk/

InteracTive: Questions Publishing
http://www.education-quest.com/
Tel: 0121-212 0919

Managing Schools Today: Questions Publishing, Tel: 0121-212 0919

Teachers:
http://www.dfee.gov.uk/teacher/index.htm

Teaching Times:
http://www.teachingtimes.com/

Technology and Learning:
http://www.techlearning.com

The following newspapers have IT-related sections:

The Daily Telegraph: 'Connected' (every Thursday)
http://www.telegraph.co.uk

The Financial Times has an IT supplement on the first Wednesday of
each month
http://www.ft.com.

The Guardian: 'Online' (every Thursday), and educ@guardian (quarterly
supplement)
http://www.guardian.co.uk

The *TES* has an occasional supplement called 'Online'
http://www.tes.co.uk

The Times: 'Interface' (every Wednesday)
http://www.the-times.co.uk

Exhibitions

The BETT Show:
http://www.education-net.co.uk/bett/

The Education Show:
http://www.education-net.co.uk/education/Seminars/index.html

Useful web sites

BECTa:
http://www.becta.org.uk
Tel: 01203 416994

BESA (British Educational Suppliers Association):
http://www.besanet.org.uk
Tel: 0171 527 4997

DfEE:
http://www.open.gov.uk/dfee/
Tel: 0171 925 5000

Government press releases:
http://www.open.gov.uk/cctagis/whatsnew.htm

HMSO:
http://www.the-stationery-office.co.uk/

NGfL:
http://www.ngfl.gov.uk/

OFSTED:
http://www.ofsted.gov.uk/
Tel: 0171 421 6800

QCA:
http://www.open.gov.uk/qca/index.htm
Tel: 0171 229 1234

SCET (Scottish Council for Educational Technology):
http://www.scet.com
Tel: 0141 337 5000

The Office of Fair Trading guide to purchasing on the internet:
http://www.oft.gov.uk/html/shopping/index.html
Tel: 0171 211 8000

The PM's Office:
http://www.number-10.gov.uk/index.html

TTA:

http://www.teach-tta.gov.uk/improve.htm

Tel: 0171 925 3728

Virtual Teachers' Centre:

http://vtc.ngfl.gov.uk/vtc/index.html

Subject organisations

ACITT (National Association for Co-ordinators and Teachers of IT):

http://www.acitt.org.uk

MAPE (Micros and Primary Education):

http://www.mape.org.uk

NAACE (National Association of Advisers for Computers in Education):

http://www.naace.org

Chapter-specific resources

Chapter 1

There is a comprehensive description of the work of the ICT Co-ordinator called Technology Co-ordinator – An Impossible Job? by Barbara Bray. Look it up at

http://www.techlearning.com/db_area/archives/WCE/archives/bray.htm.

On the subject of reducing the burden of teachers' administration, see Freedman, Terry: *Reducing the Administrative Burden – in the Classroom and Beyond, Technology and Learning*, February 1999, and Chapter 10.

Chapter 2

Mailing lists: Look at www.liszt.com for a full list of mailing lists. Also, look at www.techlearning.com for a comprehensive listing of resources.

Newsgroups: There are several useful ones, but a good starting point is the UK Education section. Have a look at uk.education.schools-it.

There are several hardware evaluation web sites, but one of the best is www.compare.net.

Chapter 3

CLA, Copyright Concerns, The Copyright Licensing Agency Ltd, September 1998. This is an excellent booklet which contains details of organisations engaged in licensing. Also, http://www.cla.co.uk.

For shareware programs web sites, look at the main search engines, such as www.yahoo.co.uk. Try www.shareware.com.

Chapter 4

OFSTED: Primary Subjects and Standards, Issues for school development arising from OFSTED inspection findings 1994-5, Key Stages 1 & 2

OFSTED: Secondary Subjects and Standards, Issues for school development arising from OFSTED inspection findings 1994-5, Key Stages 3 & 4 and Post-16, HMSO, 1996

The Annual Report of Her Majesty's Chief Inspector of Schools, Standards and Quality in Education, 1997-98, paragraph 44.

Gabriel Goldstein, Information Technology in English Schools, A commentary on inspection findings 1995-6, NCET, 1997

For furniture and other suppliers, contact BESA (British Educational Suppliers Association):
http://www.besanet.org.uk
Tel: 0171 527 4997

More health and safety information may be found at
http://www.becta.org.uk/info-sheets/hands.html.

Chapter 5

No specific resources recommended.

Chapter 6

See Delivering and assessing IT through the curriculum, published by NCET, 1998, for examples of curriculum plans for Key Stage 3.

Further information and guidance on planning for OFSTED may be found in Reviewing IT and Inspecting IT, both published by

NAACE/NCET, 1997. A good summary of the steps you need to take may be found in Doug Brown's article, The return of Ofsted, in InTeractive, October/November 1998. A very useful publication from OFSTED is Inspecting Subjects and Aspects 11-18: Information Technology (February 1999).

Further information on post-OFSTED action planning may be found in OFSTED, Planning improvement: Schools' post-inspection action plans, HMSO, 1996.

QCA/DfEE, Information Technology: A scheme of work for Key Stages 1 and 2, 1998.

Barking and Dagenham, Problem solving with IT: Year group targets for Key Stages 1 and 2, 1995.

Fenton, Paul: 'Vertical Integration', InTegrate, 22 January 1996.

Chapter 7

For further information on using a spreadsheet as a mark book, see Freedman, Terry: 'Computers – What's in it for me?' In Computers Don't Bite, BBC, 1998.

See also Information Technology: Consistency in Teacher Assessment, Exemplification of Standards, published by SCAA, 1996.

Chapter 8

See, for example, John Hobson's article, Unfair shares for all, in Educational Computing and Technology, September 1998.

For examples of some imaginative approaches, including ones that involve parents and local businesses, see the 'educ@guardian' supplement to The Guardian, 9 March 1999 (also on-line at The Guardian's web site), and Unlocking success: Lessons learned from three schools, in Technology and Learning, February 1999 (or see the magazine's web site, www.techlearning.com).

Chapter 9

For details of methods of purchasing, see the Virtual Teachers' Centre at http://vtc.ngfl.gov.uk/reference/publications/connecting/part2.2.1.html.

Managed services were suggested in Connecting the Learning Society, published by the DfEE in 1997. Further information is also available at http://vtc.ngfl.gov.uk/reference/publications/connecting/part2.2.1.html.

For a real life example of how a managed service could work, see Mr Fixit on the line, in *TES Online*, 12 February 1999.

A comprehensive list of sources of funds is available on the internet at http://vtc.ngfl.gov.uk/reference/publications/connecting/part2.2.2.html.

Chapter 10

Freedman, Terry: *Make Time With IT*, Questions Publishing, 1996, and
http://easyweb.easynet.co.uk/~etfreedman/.
Which contains a summary of each chapter of the book.

Freedman, Terry: 'Fighting the paper monster', *Managing Schools Today*, February 1999.

Freedman, Terry: 'Reducing the Administrative Burden – in the Classroom and Beyond', *Technology and Learning*, February 1999.

The DfEE's report is entitled Reducing the Bureaucratic Burden on Teachers, published by the DfEE as Research Report RR41, ISBN 0-85522-707-9. The Working Group's final report was published in January 1998, and is available on the internet via the Virtual Teachers' Centre at
http://vtc.ngfl.gov.uk/vtc/schoolman/manage.html
as indeed are other related documents.

DfEE Guidelines for Headteachers and other documents:
http://www.dfee.gov.uk/burden/index.htm

DfEE Bureaucracy Milestones:
http://www.dfee.gov.uk/burden/plan.htm

How schools might handle management activities in 2002:
http://www.dfee.gov.uk/burden/vision.htm

(See also the tools available at
http://vtc.ngfl.gov.uk/profdev/smanagers/schools/tools.html.)

See also DfEE Research Report RR41, Reducing the Bureaucratic Burden on Teachers (the Coopers and Lybrand Report)

Chapter 11

No specific resources recommended.

Chapter 12

Examination Boards:

AEB/SEG: http://www.aeb.org.uk/, Tel: 01483 506506

EdExcel: http://www.edexcel.org.uk/, Tel: 0171 393 4500

JEB: http://www.jeb.co.uk/, Tel: 01285 641747

NEAB: http://www.neab.ac.uk/, compit@neab.ac.uk

OCR: http://www.ocr.org.uk/, Tel: 01223 552552

Chapter 13

Our Information Age: see the Number-10 web site at
http://www.number-10.gov.uk/public/info/index.html

For advice on, and examples of, Acceptable Use Policies, see
http://www.esd123.wednet.edu/lk-aup.htm

BEON:
http://www.icl.fi/ajassa/clinton.htm and
http://www.tagish.co.uk/ethosub/lit6/d1de.htm.
Also, search the Virtual Teachers' Centre for the report on the Education Departments' Superhighways Initiative.

Index